the giraffe

family cookbook

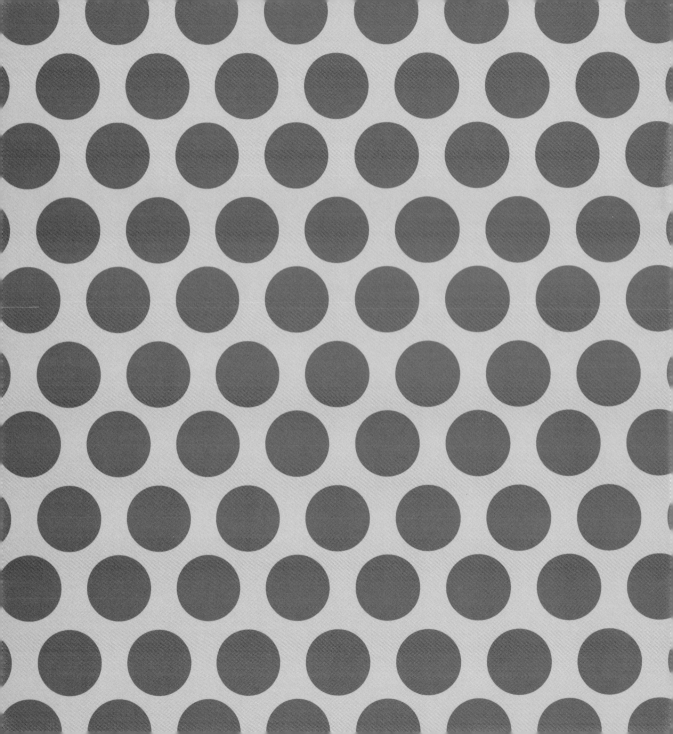

the giraffe

family cookbook

Hugo Arnold

WEIDENFELD & NICOLSON

Contents

What is global family food?

Burritos, tacos, satay, curries, jambalaya, falafel, fish with various salsa, ceviche, stacked pancakes and Asian noodles – a breathtaking array of foods, flavours and styles of cooking from around the world. Food at Giraffe is a journey to every corner of the globe. Each dish, whilst remaining true to its original culture, is given a little extra fresh-tasting twist.

Great for families as well as those keen to try something new, I created our delicious and often health-conscious recipes, with the help of consultant Hugo Arnold and my team at Giraffe, to be fun and easy to make at home. It's just the sort of food I like to cook at home for my family. I hope you will too – relax and enjoy!

RUSSEL JOFFE, FOUNDER OF GIRAFFE

1

A good morning brekkie, brunch, and sandwiches

How you start your day
says a lot about you. Modern thinking
seems too focused on the quick fix. We are a bit
old-fashioned about it really. Porridge scores highly,
pancakes are a winner and fresh fruit is hard to beat. While
we realise finding time is a challenge for all of us, occasionally
it's worth taking things a little more slowly. At the weekends maybe.

Giraffes are essentially passive creatures,
yet when you're that tall there is a lot to
think about. There is something to be
learned from this approach. A little
time out in the mornings is a good
thing, it kinda sets you up for
the day. Makes you smile.
Puts things in perspective.

ALL RECIPES SERVE 4.

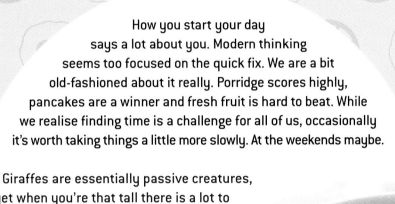

Stacked banana and blueberry pancakes with organic maple syrup

Pancakes have been on the Giraffe menu since the start. Wonderfully versatile, they work just as well with fruit as bacon. We think maple syrup is a must, regardless, but then we have a bit of a sweet tooth. We believe breakfast is an important part of the day. It may not be a particularly relaxed affair, but it is too often rushed and overlooked. Time to fuel up, with pancakes for all, toppings to be decided individually.

blueberry compote
500g blueberries
200g sugar
100ml water

280g plain flour
1 teaspoon baking powder
50g sugar
3 eggs
300ml milk
oil for cooking
4 bananas, peeled and sliced
maple syrup

1. Combine the blueberries, sugar and water, place over a low heat and simmer until the blueberries just start to collapse. Allow to cool.

2. Combine the flour, baking powder and sugar in a bowl. Mix the eggs and milk and pour into the centre of the flour. Whisk to a thick batter. You may need to add more milk.

3. Heat a non-stick frying pan, smear with oil – you really do not need much – and ladle on a little of the mixture. Cook for one minute, flip over and cook for the same time on the other side. Transfer to the oven and keep warm.

4. Slice the bananas lengthways and serve with a stack of pancakes (at least three for a decent height) and a spoonful of the blueberry compote and topped with maple syrup.

Tall tales

Other things to serve with pancakes – choose a few and serve in bowls so people can help themselves at the table:

Sliced peaches in summer
A compote of berries in the autumn
Sausages and bacon in the winter
Roast rhubarb and yoghurt in the spring
Fresh strawberries and cream
Fresh blueberries
Chocolate sauce for the kids

Ranch style eggs tostada plus options

Putting breakfast on an open tortilla is just one of those ideas that makes such perfect sense. If you are in a hurry, or just like to eat with your fingers, you can roll it up. Or settle down with a knife and fork. It's all summer sunshine, bright colours and packed full of flavour. A wake-up call to be recommended.

avocado tomato salsa

1 avocado, diced
1 beef tomato, deseeded and diced
1 small red onion, diced
2 tablespoons fresh coriander, chopped
1 clove garlic, chopped
1 spring onion, finely sliced
1 red chilli, deseeded and chopped or to taste
1 tablespoon fresh parsley, chopped
$^1/_2$ teaspoon lime juice
salt and pepper

ranch style eggs

adobe sauce
tinned black beans
8 tablespoons tinned sweetcorn, rinsed and drained
4 flour tortillas
2 chorizo sausages, thinly sliced
2 cups mixed cheddar and mozzarella cheese, grated
2 tablespoons olive oil
8 eggs
a few sprigs coriander

adobe sauce

3 tablespoon vegetable oil
100g white onions, diced
150g chopped tomatoes
25g fresh coriander, chopped
25g adobe chillies
1 teaspoon cumin powder
1 teaspoon coriander powder

1. Preheat the oven to 190C/gas mark 5.

2. Combine the salsa ingredients and season with salt and pepper.

3. Mix the adobe sauce, drained black beans and sweetcorn. Spread a thin layer of this mix on the tortilla. Place the chorizo slices on the tortilla and sprinkle the mozzarella cheese on the top. Place the tortilla on a roasting tray in the oven and cook for five to six minutes or until the cheese is bubbling. Keep warm.

4. Heat the olive oil in a frying pan and cook the eggs. Take the tortilla from the oven, put two eggs on each one and top with the avocado salsa. Garnish with fresh coriander leaves and serve.

Toasted banana sandwich with maple syrup and crispy bacon

Challah bread - also known as khale, barches, bergis and chalka in Polish - is slightly sweet, but not as sweet as brioche can be. It is a traditional Jewish bread which is plaited and eaten on the Sabbath and so leftovers are likely on Saturday morning when this is a simple, quick and easy brunch dish. Thrifty but packed with flavour. If this recipe looks a little too much for a Saturday morning try toasting and spreading with avocado and cream cheese and a good grating of salt and pepper.

8 streaky bacon rashers
1 tablespoon butter
1 tablespoon vegetable oil
4 bananas, sliced on the diagonal, about half a centimetre thick
8 slices of challah bread
maple syrup

1. Grill the bacon until crispy.

2. Combine the butter and oil in a pan over a moderate heat. Sauté the bananas quickly and set aside. Toast the bread and then fry in the butter and oil until golden, about one minute each side.

3. Layer the toasted bread and bananas and scatter the bacon over the top. Drizzle with maple syrup. Or package conventionally if you want to pick up.

Tall tales

Think maple syrup is pricy? Consider this. It takes approximately 40 litres of sap to be boiled down to 1 litre of syrup. A mature sugar maple produces about 40 litres of sap during the 4-6 week sugaring season. Trees are not tapped until they have a diameter of 25cm at chest-height and the tree is at least 40 years old ... so nothing happens fast in maple land.

French toast, poached peaches and maple syrup

500ml milk
$1/_2$ teaspoon vanilla extract
2 eggs, beaten
1 tablespoon caster sugar
50g butter
8 slices of brioche bread
150ml maple syrup
200ml créme fraiche

4 peaches, halved
300ml water
200g sugar
1 cinnamon stick
juice and zest of 1 orange
zest of 1 lemon
4 cloves
100ml white wine

1. Bring the milk and vanilla to the boil, remove from the heat and leave to cool. Whisk the eggs and combine with the cooled milk and the caster sugar.

2. Poach the peaches in a pan with all the other ingredients for 10 minutes or until soft to the touch. Remove the stones and allow to cool.

3. Heat a pan and melt the butter. Dip the brioche in the egg mixture so it is coated on both sides and transfer to the pan. Fry until golden brown and serve with the poached peaches on top, the maple syrup and créme fraiche.

French toast with crispy prosciutto

1 tablespoon olive oil
8 slices prosciutto
80g butter
3 tablespoons single cream
3 eggs
2 tablespoons sugar
1 teaspoon cinnamon
8 thick slices of challah bread
maple syrup to serve

1. Heat a frying pan over a moderate heat and add the olive oil. Fry the prosciutto on both sides until crispy. Remove and drain on kitchen paper. Add the butter to the pan and remove from the heat.

2. Combine the cream, eggs, sugar and cinnamon and whisk. Return the pan to the heat. Dip the bread in the egg mixture and fry until golden brown. Keep warm until you use up all the bread.

3. Serve the fried bread with the crispy bacon and a generous drizzle of maple syrup.

Brekkie burrito

Breakfast is different for everyone, that is part of its attraction. Here we've added a slightly unconventional mixture of Mexican-style ingredients to eggs. Healthy? Well, while it is not exactly thin-food, it is all fresh and there is minimum cooking and not quite as much focus on meat as your traditional fry-up.

2 cooking chorizo, sliced
8 eggs, lightly whisked
150g tomatoes, chopped
$1/2$ teaspoon paprika
Chilli pepper flakes to taste,
    sprinkling
4 tortillas
8 slices Monterey Jack cheese
1 avocado, diced
2 handfuls rocket
olive oil

1. Preheat the oven to 180C/gas mark 4.

2. Heat a frying pan over a moderate heat. When hot add the chorizo and fry until lightly coloured. Turn over and repeat on the other side. Add the egg, season with salt and pepper and cook through, stirring occasionally. Stir in the tomatoes, paprika and a ¼ teaspoon of chilli flakes – it depends how you like chilli, but it gives a nice morning wake up!

3. Divide the mixture and spoon into the centre of four tortillas. Fold. Place two slices of the cheese on each tortilla and transfer to the oven. Bake for five minutes or until the cheese has melted.

4. Toss the avocado with the rocket and two tablespoons of olive oil and a seasoning of salt. Place on top of the burritos and serve.

Tall tales

Chorizo varies enormously in quality and it is well worth searching out something from a good quality delicatessen.

Granola sundae

This may look like an indulgent calorie-rich treat but is actually loaded with health and goodness in the shape of granola, fresh fruit and yoghurt. So haul out those tall old-fashioned glasses and layer away for a scoop of summer sunshine.

2 bananas, sliced
2 red apples, diced
100g black grapes, cut in half
2 small kiwis, diced
8 strawberries, cut in half
1 lime
200g granola or museli
300g low-fat yoghurt or Greek
    style yoghurt
as much honey as you like

1. Prepare all the fruits and mix them in a bowl. Squeeze the lime juice over the fruit and toss all together. Best to serve in a sundae glass or bowl. Place 25g granola in a sundae glass, and then add the mixed fruits on it. Pour some yoghurt on the fruits. Drizzle some honey and add another 25g granola crunchy on the top. Finish it with a drizzle of honey.

Tall tales

Honey is the one food which never spoils. It literally goes on forever. There are examples of honey being found hundreds of years after it was buried in clay pots. Real natural goodness.

Can't find the fruits listed here? The idea is to use this as a guide. Look for fruits in season that have contrasting textures and flavours; dates, orange segments and pineapple work well in winter for example.

Fried halloumi, vine tomato and rocket in seeded ciabatta roll

Vegetarian dishes that are not pasta or risotto are a hard nut to crack for many chefs. This was a lunch special one week and became such a firm favourite it has returned many times since. It's a fairly superior sandwich, or a hearty lunch, whichever way you prefer to look at it.

400g halloumi cheese, thickly sliced
juice of 1 lemon
1 garlic clove, peeled and crushed
1 dessertspoon dried capers, chopped
4 tablespoons olive oil
4 ciabatta rolls
12 vine tomatoes, thickly sliced
bunch fresh basil leaves
4 handfuls rocket
salt and pepper

1. Grill or pan-fry the halloumi. Whisk together the lemon juice, garlic and capers with the olive oil and pour over the cheese.

2. Warm the ciabatta in the oven. Halve the ciabatta and put the cheese on the bottom slice of bread and top with the tomatoes, basil leaves and rocket. Season with salt and pepper.

3. Spoon over any of the remaining dressing and place the top slice of the roll over everything.

Our favourite BLT fried egg and cheese toastie

Sometimes a big breakfast is really what everyone wants. Including you. The default option may be the big fry but a plate of these to hand round can be equally satisfying and they are decidedly portable. Just the thing when there is a football match on the TV, or when minds are busy on other things. A pot of coffee makes for a complete picture.

8 slices streaky bacon
2 tablespoon mayonnaise
English mustard
8 slices aged cheddar
8 slices sourdough bread, toasted
4 eggs
4 tomatoes, sliced
lettuce

1. Heat a frying pan over a medium heat. When hot, add the bacon and fry for five minutes each side, turning at least twice until cooked to your liking. Drain on kitchen paper and set aside. Keep the pan and bacon fat.

2. Spread mayonnaise and a little English mustard on one side of the toast and top with the bacon and cheese. Return the frying pan to the heat and when hot break the eggs into the bacon fat. Fry, turning once, until cooked. Place on top of the cheese. Layer the tomatoes and lettuce, top with the remaining slice of bread and serve.

BBQ chicken and smoked cheddar quesadilla

You could call this a toastie, or cheese on toast, or warm bread with cheese and something. There is something all-encompassing about a quesadilla. Originally the stuffing was cheese and nothing else but things have moved on a little bit. Which is lucky really as half the fun is working on the combinations. We are also keen on spinach and cheese, or rocket, chorizo and créme fraiche. We even tried steak once, but it didn't quite work, something about the thickness of the meat was wrong. Stick to simple combinations, however, and it is hard to go wrong.

300g cooked chicken, sliced
100g BBQ sauce
200g tinned sweetcorn
200g tinned black beans
200g adobe sauce
  (see page 13)
4 flour tortillas
2 spring onions finely sliced
200g smoked cheddar, grated
100g mozzarella, grated
100g mayonnaise
100g soured cream
2 tablespoons chipotle Tabasco

tomato salsa
4 beef tomatoes, core and
  seeds removed
1 small red onion, peeled and
  finely diced
1 bunch each fresh coriander
  and parsley, roughly chopped
1 garlic clove, peeled and
  chopped
1 red chilli, trimmed and finely
  diced
juice and zest of 1 lime
salt and pepper

*Combine all the ingredients,
season with salt and pepper
and leave aside for 10 minutes.*

1. Slice the cooked chicken and toss it with BBQ sauce. Add the sweetcorn and black beans to the adobe sauce. Spread the sauce mix on one half of each of the flour tortillas. Add the BBQ chicken, half the tomato salsa, spring onions and sprinkle the smoked cheddar and mozzarella on top.

2. Fold the tortilla to make a half-moon shape. Fry in a scant tablespoon of oil in a hot non-stick frying pan over a moderate heat for two minutes or until it crisps up. Turn over and repeat on the other side ensuring the cheese is melted.

3. Mix the mayonnaise, soured cream and chipotle Tabasco to make chipotle aioli. Cut the quesadilla in three pieces and serve with chipotle aioli and tomato salsa.

Tall tales

Chipotle chillies have a gentle smoky flavour. You can use ordinary Tabasco but it really is not quite the same thing.

Open Mediterranean BLT bruschetta

Cheese and ham on toast doesn't have quite the same ring to it as bruschetta but that really is the essence of this simple but stylish way with bread and bright summery ingredients. You could of course put a top on it and make it closed. Useful if you plan to eat it with your fingers. But this way makes for something altogether more elegant. With a glass of fresh juice, you've got a pretty healthy lunch, or supper, or snack.

2 garlic cloves, 1 peeled and thinly sliced
6 ripe vine tomatoes, halved
salt and pepper
1 teaspoon dried oregano
olive oil
4 slices from a good quality, crusty white loaf
4 slices Provalone cheese
4 slices Bayonne ham
4 handfuls rocket
handful basil leaves
1 tablespoon balsamic vinegar

1. Preheat the oven to 180C/gas mark 4. Insert a slither of garlic into each of the tomato halves. Season with salt and pepper, scatter over the oregano and drizzle over a few tablespoons of olive oil. Roast in the oven for 20 minutes, remove and set aside

2. Toast the bread, rub with the remaining clove of garlic and drizzle with olive oil.

3. Build your bruschetta with cheese, ham, rocket and tomatoes. Scatter over the basil and drizzle more oil and a little balsamic vinegar.

Tall tales

You can slow roast tomatoes overnight in a very low oven. If you do this the liquid largely evaporates and the flavour is concentrated to give you something akin to sun-dried tomatoes, only fresher.

Goat's cheese focaccia

There are times when a sandwich is just the thing; easy to make, convenient to eat and, when well made, delicious. Where a bought sandwich made in a factory and chilled within an inch of its life is, well, pretty tasteless, a home-made sandwich can deliver plenty of oomph.

1 red pepper
2 courgettes, sliced lengthways
olive oil
salt and pepper
1 round or square focaccia measuring 30cm or so in diameter
2 garlic cloves, peeled and crushed with a little salt
200g goat's cheese, thinly sliced
1 beef tomato, cored and sliced
4/5 leaves lettuce, shredded

1. Preheat the grill or better still, a ridged griddle pan. Cook the pepper until well charred on all sides, remove to a bowl, cover with clingfilm or a damp cloth and set aside.

2. Lightly brush the courgettes with oil, season with salt and pepper and grill on both sides for two to three minutes or until charred and tender. Add to the red pepper.

3. Preheat the oven to 150C/gas mark 2. Cut the focaccia in two horizontally and drizzle the cut sides with olive oil and spread the garlic paste as evenly as you can. Slice the goat's cheese and scatter over the bottom half of the focaccia. Place in the oven to melt the cheese – you want it soft but not too gooey.

4. Peel the pepper, discard the seeds and tear into strips. Remove the bottom half of the focaccia from the oven, layer the pepper and courgettes on top, followed by the tomato and lettuce seasoning as you go. Drizzle with more olive oil and add the top half of the focaccia. Cut into quarters and serve. We typically serve this with potato wedges but at home a packet of good crisps is perhaps a little easier.

Tall tales

A good splash of chilli sauce will liven things up. Beetroot brings both colour and attitude. Summer herbs like basil and tarragon will brighten things considerably. And a good spread of pesto in the winter will hint at a ray of sunshine.

Steak sandwich with hummus and salad

Mayo is something of a default for many when it comes to sandwiches. Russel's son Gideon has a thing about hummus. In his view it goes with pretty much everything and is perfect in a steak sandwich. Certainly from a health perspective it works, but as the juices from the meat mix with the hummus and bread there is decided lickability with everything. A true sandwich — one of the greats.

2 tablespoons olive oil
$^1/_2$ teaspoon Dijon mustard
$^1/_2$ teaspoon red wine vinegar
1 small garlic clove, peeled and
   crushed
salt and pepper

4 Romaine lettuce leaves, shredded
4 radicchio leaves, shredded
4 100g minute steaks
4 ciabatta rolls or crusty baguettes
4 tablespoons hummus
2 plum tomatoes, cored and sliced
1 ripe avocado, sliced

1. Preheat and griddle pan or frying pan.

2. Combine the olive oil, mustard, vinegar and garlic with a seasoning of salt and pepper. Toss with the salad leaves.

3. Season the steaks and grill for two minutes either side for rare, three minutes for medium.

4. Warm or toast the rolls. Spread half the hummus on the bottom slice of each roll. Lay the steak on top, and layer avocado and tomatoes on top of the steak. Finish with the salad and spread the remainder of the hummus on the top slice of bread.

5. Serve with more salad or with fried potatoes or homemade sweet potato chips.

Tall tales

Who is Russel?

Russel founded Giraffe with his wife Juliette. He is an avid home cook and likes nothing more than to be behind the stove, particularly at the weekend when family and friends gather to talk and eat. It is this approach that informs much of what Giraffe does; simple tasty food in relaxed, friendly surroundings.

Hot dog in a soft bun with chow-chow relish

While burgers have soared in popularity over recent years the hot dog has been rather left behind. Which is a shame as the spiced pork sausage is a great partner to so many other ingredients. Good value eating. The chow-chow in the relish refers to the sweet and sour aspect and often includes vegetables either chopped or cut into thin strips.

chow chow relish
2 onions, peeled and sliced
2 jalapeño peppers, trimmed and
    chopped (or to taste)
4 tablespoons cider vinegar
2 tablespoons olive oil
2 tablespoons soft brown sugar
1 tablespoon English mustard
t teaspoon caraway seeds
1 teaspoon turmeric
salt and pepper

4 hot dogs or sausages
4 soft hot dog buns

1. Lightly sauté the onions and jalapeños in the olive oil over a moderate heat for 10 minutes. Add the cider vinegar, brown sugar, mustard, caraway seeds and turmeric. Mix, season and simmer until the mixture thickens, about 10 minutes. Check seasoning.

2. Cook the hot dogs or sausages and serve with the chow chow relish in the bun or on the side.

2

Sharing for all the family – a great way to start

For all the excitement
and attraction of individual servings,
there is nothing to quite beat the thrill of a
table full of different dishes. What to have first, how to
combine, whether to have one dish before or after another...

This chapter is about the art of sharing, a way to start which
doesn't need to be overly concerned about the likes and dislikes of
everyone sitting around the table. A wide choice will ensure satisfaction.

Think colour as well as texture and flavour. You want to introduce
difference and contrast so each person can choose for themselves.

What to combine with what is never easy. But having four or five dishes
means you don't have to worry too much. And don't feel
you have to do everything from scratch. You might
choose to do the grilled avocado and combine
it with some bottled grilled vegetables and
cold meats. The aim is not to cook for
hours, but to chill out.

ALL RECIPES SERVE 4.

Edamame with soy, ginger and chilli

You can buy edamame – literally soy beans in their pods – frozen from good supermarkets. Once cooked and seasoned you then eat them with your fingers, pushing the beans from their pods into your mouth. The resulting tangy taste of chilli and garlic with soy and the odd crunch of sea salt is one of life's little pleasures that delivers rather a lot of satisfaction. At least we giraffes like to think so. But then we are quite simple folk really.

500g edamame (or muki beans)
1 tablespoon ginger and chilli paste
1 tablespoon teriyaki sauce
Maldon sea salt

1. Bring enough water to cover the edamame to the boil in a wok or large pan. Add the beans, return to the boil and simmer for two minutes. Drain.

2. Add the ginger and chilli paste and the teryaki sauce to the wok and toss so the edamame are well coated.

3. Transfer into two bowls and season with the salt.

Tall tales

It is not often we specify something like salt to this extent. But Maldon (a town in Essex on the east coast of the UK) produces a salt which really is quite unique. It is not just the flavour – think fresh, tangy sea spray – but the consistency; light and feathery, a sort of elegant crunch.

Ginger and chilli paste can be found in ethnic stores. The ginger and chilli is suspended in oil and flavoured with other ingredients, depending on the brand.

Chicken gourmet nuggets with blue cheese and BBQ dip

Fast food has something of a bad reputation but it is possible to have good healthy food, fast. Which is what Giraffe likes to do. No fuss, no frills, but quite a lot of attention to the detail. These nuggets are great for parties as they are easy finger food.

4 chicken breasts, cut into nugget-sized pieces
salt and pepper
plain flour
2 eggs, beaten
4 heaped tablespoons breadcrumbs or panko crumbs
1 teaspoon dried oregano
vegetable oil for frying

BBQ dip
1 tablespoon red wine vinegar
1 tablespoon honey
$1/2$ teaspoon cayenne pepper or to taste
1 tablespoon Dijon mustard
2 tablespoons tomato ketchup

blue cheese sauce
4 tablespoons Greek-style yoghurt
100g blue cheese, crumbled (ideally something like Blue d'Avergne or similar. Stilton tends to go crumbly)
$1/2$ small red onion, peeled and grated
bunch flat leaf parsley, chopped
salt and pepper

1. Season the chicken. Season the flour. Dip the chicken nuggets in the flour, then in the egg, then in the breadcrumbs and oregano.

2. Combine the ingredients for the BBQ dip, mix to taste and set aside.

3. Combine the ingredients for the blue cheese sauce, season and set aside.

4. Heat enough oil to just cover the nuggets and when hot fry the nuggets until golden brown, turning once or twice. You will need to do this in batches so drain on kitchen paper and keep warm.

5. Alternatively preheat the oven to 200C/gas mark 6. Spread the nuggets out on a baking tray, lightly drizzle with oil and bake for 20-30 minutes or until brown and cooked through.

6. Serve on a large oval dish with cocktail sticks and the two dipping sauces.

Tall tales

Salmon makes an equally good nugget, tuna too. Or try some fillet steak cubed. You see fast food really can be good food.

Although darker, the thigh meat of chicken is more succulent. The same is true of the wing meat. Both of these cuts tend to be less expensive than breast meat.

Raw Asian salad with Thai dressing

Flavours from the East, crunchy vegetables and no cooking: what could be healthier, more refreshing, or more satisfying? There is plenty of ying and yang in this salad, the satisfaction in the checks and balances. Go on, be a good giraffe and eat up your greens with a difference.

100g red cabbage
100g white cabbage
100g carrots
1 green, 1 red and 1 yellow pepper, deseeded
100g romaine lettuce
50g rocket leaves
100g radicchio leaves
100g French beans
100g podded edamame

Thai dressing
6 tablespoons soy sauce
2 tablespoons fish sauce
1 tablespoon oyster sauce
1 tablespoon chilli sauce
2 garlic cloves, peeled, finely chopped and mashed with a little salt
1 tablespoon sugar
juice of 1 lime
pinch black pepper

1. Finely shred the red and white cabbage and carrots. Julienne the red, green and yellow peppers.

2. Wash the salad leaves and roughly chop. Trim the stem end of the French beans and blanch in boiling salted water, drain and refresh under cold water. Combine the peppers, beans, cabbage and carrots with the edamame and salad leaves.

3. Mix all the dressing ingredients together. Toss the salad leaves and all vegetables with the dressing and season with salt and pepper.

4. This salad is also a good accompaniment for grilled fish.

Tandoori chicken skewers with cucumber raita

A tandoor oven is something to behold; build of clay and with a fierce heat it cooks meat to a golden mouthwatering succulent finish. The spicing associated with this style of cooking are used here with chicken skewers to give you a taste of what you might get in an outside cafe in India. Evocative, healthy, simple and good.

2 tablespoons curry powder
$^1/_2$ teaspoon cayenne pepper
$^1/_2$ teaspoon sweet paprika
$^1/_2$ teaspoon turmeric
$^1/_2$ teaspoon ground cumin powder
$^1/_2$ teaspoon ground coriander
4 garlic cloves, peeled, finely chopped and mashed with a little salt
3cm piece of ginger, peeled and grated
2 tablespoons fresh coriander, roughly chopped
juice of 1 lemon
6 tablespoons Greek yoghurt
4 chicken breasts
olive oil
wooden skewers, soaked in warm water for 20 minutes

raita
1 cucumber, deseeded and finely diced
2 tablespoons mint, finely chopped
2 tablespoons fresh coriander, roughly chopped
1 teaspoon sugar
250g Greek yoghurt
salt and pepper

1. Mix all the spices, garlic, ginger, coriander and lemon juice into the yoghurt. Cut the chicken breast into strips and mix it well with yoghurt. Leave for two to three hours and then thread on to skewers.

2. Mix all the ingredients for the raita together and season with salt and pepper.

3. Preheat the grill. Drain the excess marinade from the chicken skewers, drizzle with a little olive oil and grill until lightly charred and cooked through, about two minutes each side.

4. Serve with cold cucumber raita.

Grilled tuna skewers with yakitori-style dip and pea-shoot salad

As giraffes we are very conscious of sustainability. Clearing the oceans is not a good idea. Sustainable yellowfin tuna is what we mean here by tuna. If you are finding sustainable tuna hard to find this also works well with monkfish, line-caught monkfish that is. Give the fish a chance and we can all live in a happy world.

200ml light soy sauce
100ml mirin (sweet rice wine)
100ml rice wine vinegar
2 cloves garlic, peeled and grated
1 teaspoon freshly grated ginger
1 tablespoon brown sugar
2 x 225g tuna steaks (cubed) (or 4 x 225g steaks if for a main course)
4 generous handfuls of a mixture of pea shoots, watercress and lettuce
1 scant tablespoon toasted sesame seeds

1. Combine all the yakitori ingredients in a saucepan, bring to the boil, lower the heat and simmer for five minutes. Allow to cool.

2. Combine the tuna with half of the yakitori sauce, toss gently but thoroughly, and set aside for just 20 minutes. Don't leave any longer or the marinade will start to 'cook' the tuna.

3. Soak 12cm wooden skewers in warm water for 20 minutes. Thread the tuna on to the skewers and grill for one minute on each side.

4. Serve on top of the pea shoots with a scattering of sesame seeds and the remains of the yakitori sauce to dip into.

Tall tales

Sesame seeds are far better bought untoasted and done to order. Heat a dry frying pan over a moderate heat and when good and hot add the sesame seeds. Toss lightly and watch them closely as they burn easily. Transfer to a plate and allow to cool.

Prawn cocktail with chipotle spiced sauce and tortilla chips

The rise in popularity of classics like prawn cocktail is one of the most welcome aspects of the vibrant food culture in the UK today. Made well, it is a great dish. While a Marie Rose sauce may be more authentic, this slight twist gives it an edge which is both welcome and exciting.

500g cooked peeled prawns
2 plum tomatoes, cut in wedges
2 tablespoons fresh lemon
    or lime juice
1 avocado, cut into cubes
salt and pepper
$1/4$ iceberg lettuce, shredded
$1/4$ red onion, peeled and sliced thinly
4 lemon wedges
chilli tortilla chips

chipotle spiced sauce
250ml mayonnaise
2 tablespoons tomato ketchup
1 teaspoon Lea and Perrin's
    Worcestershire sauce
2 chipotle chillies, deseeded and
    finely chopped (or dried and
    soaked in warm water, chopped)
$1/2$ teaspoon paprika
splash of Tabasco
1 lemon, zested and juiced
1 tablespoon of coriander, chopped
salt and pepper

1. Combine the first four ingredients, season with salt and pepper and toss lightly.

2. Toss the iceberg and red onion with a seasoning of salt and pepper and distribute into four glasses or bowls. Spoon the prawn mixture on top of the lettuce and top with the chipotle sauce. Serve with lemon wedges and tortilla chips

Tall tales

If you combine the sliced red onion with a teaspoon of salt in a sieve and toss lightly the strength of the onions is reduced and they taste less 'raw'. Leave for five minutes and rinse under plenty of cold water.

Other things to do with chipotle spiced sauce:

Use in place of tartar sauce with fried fish
Use to make a fiery potato salad

Sticky jerk BBQ chicken drumsticks

Giraffes are inveterate nibblers. It's just what they do. It may be leaves for our tall-necked cousins but we rather favour the likes of these drumsticks along with the nuggets on page 32.

Good fast food is all in the execution, and who is doing the cooking. Fast food, cooked freshly at home is hard to better. Good stuff in, good stuff out. This BBQ sauce has a freshness and vitality to it. Something worth finger licking for.

BBQ sauce
300ml tomato ketchup
1 tablespoon honey
1 tablespoon dark brown sugar
1 tablespoon Worcestershire sauce
2 teaspoons mustard
1 tablespoon lime juice
generous pinch jerk seasoning (see page 114)

12 chicken drumsticks
salt and pepper
olive oil
3 limes, quartered

1. Combine all the barbecue sauce ingredients in a small saucepan over a low heat and simmer until everything is amalgamated. Allow to cool.

2. Keep a little of the sauce back for dipping and then toss the drumsticks in the remaining BBQ sauce. The easiest – and messiest – way to do this is with your hands but it really does help to coat the chicken well.

3. Preheat the oven to 180C/gas mark 4 or fire up your barbecue. Season the drumsticks with salt and pepper and drizzle with olive oil. Bake for 20-25 minutes or until golden brown. Allow to cool and serve with lots of paper towels, a little extra barbecue sauce for dipping and lime wedges.

4. Serve with salad or jacket potatoes.

Flat mushrooms, goat's cheese, garlic and chilli

Garlic mushrooms are one of those timeless classics that always seem to surf between comfort food and something so retro they are completely up to date. Top with goat's cheese and a scoop of salsa and things really begin to take off.

16 flat mushrooms, stalks removed
salt and pepper
4 tablespoons olive oil
2 garlic cloves, peeled and chopped
1 red chilli, trimmed and finely
  chopped
400g goat's cheese
4 pitta breads
$^1/_2$ teaspoon dried oregano

herb and chilli salsa
100ml olive oil
1 red onion, peeled and finely
  chopped
3 sun-dried tomatoes, finely chopped
1 red chilli, trimmed and finely
  chopped
bunch basil, finely chopped
1 garlic clove, peeled and finely
  chopped
2 teaspoons fresh oregano leaves
juice of half a lemon
1 teaspoon balsamic vinegar

*Mix all the ingredients together and
season with salt and pepper.*

1. Preheat the grill. Season the insides of the mushrooms with salt and pepper and divide the olive oil, garlic and chilli. Grill, open side up, for 12-15 minutes or until the mushrooms are soft and juicy.

2. Divide the goat's cheese between the mushrooms and return to the grill until brown and bubbling. Drizzle a little olive oil over the pitta breads, sprinkle over the oregano and flash under the grill till warmed. Serve with a rocket salad and the herb and chilli salsa.

Tall tales

If you are doing this for a party then the mushrooms can be prepared in advance as far as adding the goat's cheese. Do this and refrigerate until needed. Allow to return to room temperature and then grill and serve.

Good goat's cheese makes all the difference.

Ceviche salad Miami style

Ceviche is a way to 'cook'; in an acid bath and usually with citrus fruit, which works particularly well with fish. The result is incredibly refreshing, a sort of no-cook cooking which leaves the ingredients to do the talking. You can increase the time the fish is marinated which will firm it up but don't leave it too long or it is likely to get tough. Why Miami? Because this dish is all sun-washed and about the joys of the ocean.

juice of two limes
2 garlic cloves, peeled and finely chopped
handful fresh coriander, plus a little extra for garnishing
1 green chilli, finely chopped, or to taste
500g fresh firm white fish, skinned (sea bass, snapper, mackerel, salmon, tuna) cut into 2cm cubes
salt and pepper
1 avocado, peeled, stoned and diced
2 passion fruit, flesh scooped out
1 mango, peeled and chopped
8 cos lettuce, leaves separated
4 spring onions, trimmed and cut on the diagonal
handful flat leaf parsley

1. Combine the lime juice, garlic, coriander and chilli in a food processor and blitz briefly. Combine with the fish in a bowl, season with salt and set aside, for two hours, less if you don't want the fish quite so 'cooked'.

2. Pour off half the liquid. Add the avocado, passionfruit pulp, mango and season with salt and pepper. Lay lettuce leaves on four plates, spoon the fish mixture into the middle and garnish with the spring onions, parsley and reserved coriander.

Spinach and halloumi cakes with spiced tomato and currant chutney

Halloumi lends itself particularly well to cooking. Unlike most cheeses it doesn't melt as soon as heat is applied but goes soft while holding its shape. You often see it grilled in salads but here we grate it to make it into a rather delicious cake. You could say a veggie fishcake, but that seems rather unfair to both vegetables and halloumi.

spiced tomato and currant chutney
1 large tomato
1 red onion, finely chopped
oil for cooking
2 garlic cloves, peeled and finely
    chopped
1 small red chilli, trimmed and
    finely chopped
4 tablespoons cider vinegar
4 tablespoons soft brown sugar
5 tablespoons currants
1 tablespoon mint, chopped

400g couscous
8 tablespoons carrot, grated
120g raw baby spinach
pinch cayenne pepper
pinch turmeric
2 tablespoons each chopped mint
    and coriander
400g grated halloumi
juice of half a lemon
salt and pepper
plain flour
vegetable oil for frying

1. For the chutney, plunge the tomato into boiling water for 30 seconds, drain and remove the skin. Cut into quarters, remove the seeds, discard and roughly chop the flesh.

2. Gently sauté the onion, without colouring in the oil, for 10 minutes over a low heat. Add the garlic and chilli, cook for two minutes and then add the vinegar, sugar, currants and four tablespoons of water. Season with salt and pepper and cook for five minutes, or until thick and jam-like in consistency. When cool stir in the chopped tomato and mint and check seasoning.

3. Add an equal volume of boiling water to the couscous. Leave to stand for one minute and then stir in the carrot, spinach, cayenne and turmeric. Leave aside for two minutes. Stir in the herbs, halloumi and lemon juice and season with salt and pepper.

4. Mould into eight cakes while still warm. Dip in flour and shallow fry over a moderate heat for two minutes each side or until golden brown and heated through.

5. Serve with the chutney and a rocket salad.

Fiery chilli chicken wings

Finger lickin' good these wings certainly are. The truth is fried chicken is just such a winner; succulent chicken, a touch of spiciness and reaching for a cold beer or soft drink is as automatic as nibbling away at the branches of tall trees. The spicing here is very simple, chilli hot with lime is a Korean way while a Spanish theme creeps in with the paprika. If that all sounds a little too much of a serious chill out, why not try them and go easy on the chilli.

fiery chilli marinade
Juice of 2 limes
1 tablespoon chilli flakes, or to taste
1 tablespoon paprika
sea salt
vegetable oil

16 chicken wings
1 lime, cut into wedges

1. Mix the lime juice and chilli flakes with the paprika and sea salt and add the wings. Mix well and marinate for one hour.

2. Preheat the oven to 200C/gas mark 6. Drizzle a couple of tablespoons of oil over the wings, toss and lay out on a baking tray.

3. Bake for 20-30 minutes or until golden brown and bubbling. Serve with lime wedges and sea salt to dip into.

Tall tales

Like these? Chicken wings are incredibly versatile and lend themselves to all sorts of different flavours. The following are just a few alternatives we occasionally consider. Although to be honest there is generally a firm lament from customers who ask us to stick with the original recipe. Sometimes simple really is best.

Chinese

Combine one stick of cinnamon bark with three star anise, three slices of ginger, a strip of orange peel, three tablespoons honey, two tablespoons dark soy sauce and two tablespoons white wine vinegar with 300ml of water and boil down to a syrup. Coat chicken wings in the same. Allow to marinate and then drizzle with vegetable oil and bake as above.

Indian

Four tablespoons full-fat yoghurt combined with a teaspoon garam masala, three tablespoons vegetable oil, half a teaspoon each of cinnamon and cayenne pepper, a garlic clove peeled and crushed with a little salt and a teaspoon of turmeric. Marinate the chicken for a few hours or overnight if possible and bake in the oven as above.

Beetroot carpaccio with fresh goat's cheese, lamb's lettuce and Belgian endive

Beetroot and goat's cheese is just one of those magical combinations that works. This is a starter or lunch dish you can rustle up literally in moments. With a touch of seasoning and scant dressing of leaves all is revealed in its colourful glory.

3 medium cooked beetroot
1 teaspoon red wine vinegar
3 tablespoons olive oil
175g lamb's lettuce
1 Belgian endive, shredded
110g goat's cheese
salt and pepper

1. Slice the beetroot as thinly as you can. Toss with the vinegar, olive oil and a seasoning of salt and pepper.

2. Divide onto four plates.

3. Combine the lamb's lettuce and endive and toss together with salt and pepper. Place on top of the beetroot.

4. Sprinkle over the goat's cheese and serve.

Tall tales

A mandolin is like a mini slicer, allowing you to produce consistently thin slices of pretty much any vegetable. They are not particularly expensive unless you opt for a professional stainless steel version.

Sunshine open-faced bruschetta

Mention Greece and immediately images of blue skies, deep clear seas and lots of sunshine float into view. It's a happy feeling, something we feel positive about. Smiling is infectious; something to be encouraged. Open sandwiches are easy and this one is all about sunshine.

1 red pepper, cut into quarters
4 slices sourdough bread
1 garlic clove, halved
olive oil
8 slices halloumi cheese
4 generous scoops hummus
4 generous scoops tzatziki
4 handfuls rocket
2 Lebanese cucumbers, grated
2 tablespoons stoned kalamata olives
4 bottled artichokes, quartered
    lengthwise
1 avocado, stoned and sliced
$1/2$ lemon
salt and pepper

1. Preheat the grill. When hot place the pepper, skin side up, underneath and cook until charred. Remove to a bowl, cover with clingfilm and set aside. When cool enough to handle, remove the skin and discard. Tear into strips.

2. Grill the bread. Rub with the cut side of garlic. Place each one on a separate plate and drizzle with a little olive oil. Place the cheese under the grill and turn when it starts to blister and colour. Repeat on the other side.

3. Meanwhile pile the hummus and tzatziki on the grilled bread and top with the rocket, cucumber, olives, artichokes and avocado. Drizzle over more oil, add the lemon juice, season with salt and pepper and top with the cheese, rocket and red pepper.

Tall tales

Halloumi is a creamy white semi-hard cheese made from goat's or ewe's milk. It keeps its shape well when grilled - the heat enhances its flavour (see Spinach and Halloumi cakes on page 43 if you don't believe us). Originally made by the Bedouin in the Middle East, its good keeping qualities made it ideal for their nomadic lifestyle. We like it because it tastes great. Somewhere between feta and a creamy goat's cheese.

Other things to do with halloumi:

Try a slice on a grilled mushroom sandwich for added richness

Or add to cubed watermelon, toasted pine nuts and lots of torn mint leaves for a refreshing summer salad

Or sprinkle cubes of halloumi over a salad of halved cherry tomatoes, diced onion and garlic, lemon juice and olive oil, a tin or two of well-rinsed lentils and roughly chopped coriander

Panamanisan beef empanada

You might say the South American equivalent of a Cornish pasty. But that would be unfair to both. The former is smaller, more of a snack than a meal, the latter much rubbished by being hijacked and done badly out of itself; a rather extraordinarily wonderful package of goodness. Like so much, the devil lies in the detail.

1 large onion, diced
3 tablespoons vegetable oil
3 cloves garlic, finely chopped
1 celery stick, diced
100g chestnut mushroom, sliced
$^1/_2$ teaspoon cayenne pepper
1 teaspoon cumin
1 teaspoon ground coriander
400g ground beef
15g fresh coriander leaves, chopped
100g chopped tomatoes
1 tablespoon tomato paste
salt and pepper

100g flour
1 egg
2 tablespoons beef suet
pinch salt
1 teaspoon vinegar
$^1/_2$ cup water
vegetable oil for frying

1. For the empanada mix, sauté the onion in hot oil for two to three minutes. Add the chopped garlic, celery, chestnut mushrooms and spices. Cook, stirring occasionally, for a couple of minutes. Then add the minced beef and cook, stirring occasionally, for 20-25 minutes. Add the fresh coriander, chopped tomato and tomato paste, and season with salt and pepper. Reduce over a moderate heat so the mixture is moist but not dry.

2. Place the flour in a bowl and mix with the egg, suet and salt. Make a well in the flour mix, pour the vinegar and water and mix to a soft dough and place in fridge for an hour.

3. Roll the dough into a thin sheet and cut into 6cm diameter discs. Take the small round empanada sheet, place two teaspoons of beef mixture and fold over the sheet to close the empanada. Dampen the edges and use a fork to seal by pressing against the edges of the sheet.

4. Heat the vegetable oil and when hot, but not smoking, deep-fry the empanadas in batches in the hot oil until golden brown. Drain on kitchen paper and serve.

Tall tales

These can also be baked in a hot oven. Brush with oil and bake in a preheated oven, 200C/gas mark 6. Spread out on a tray with plenty of space in between and bake for 20-25 minutes or until golden brown.

Grilled avocado, shrimp and mango salsa

Like many great classics the combination of avocado and prawn is a real winner. Never ones to try things unchallenged we spent some time looking at a way to pep things up and this mango salsa was the result of all the hard work. Packed with zip, zing and zest, it takes a sixties dinner party dish to a new level. Just the sort of level a hungry giraffe finds comfortable.

450g cooked shrimp or tiger prawns
1 mango, stoned and cut into 0.5 centimetre dice
¹/₂ a red onion, finely diced
bunch coriander, roughly chopped
bunch flat leaf parsley, finely chopped
¹/₂ green chilli, finely chopped
Tabasco to taste
juice of 2 oranges
juice of 2 limes
salt and pepper

2 Hass avocadoes
2 limes, halved
olive oil
1 teaspoon toasted cumin seeds
1 lime to serve

1. Preheat the grill.

2. Combine all the shrimps with the mango, red onion, coriander and parsley, chilli, Tabasco to taste and the juice of the two oranges and limes. Season with salt and pepper and toss well.

3. Halve the avocados and rub with the cut limes. Drizzle over a little olive oil and scatter over the cumin seeds. Season with salt and pepper and grill for a few minutes, until just lightly coloured and blistered. Place on four plates and fill with the salsa mix to overflowing. Serve with a lime wedge.

Tall tales

An avocado has the highest protein content of any fruit.

If you want to prepare this in advance, combine the salsa ingredients but leave out the coriander and parsley. The acid from the oranges and limes will turn the herbs brown. All the other ingredients have a chance to get to know each other and the herbs will bring a bright freshness when added at the last moment.

Cheesy spinach and artichoke fondue dip with tortilla chips

One bowl, a hot cheese mixture, crunchy artichokes and spinach – retro food rarely gets this good. With a glass of wine and good company, this is a great way to start things off. A casual, easy, snack approach: very Giraffe.

200g cream cheese
150g Parmesan cheese, grated
200g Monterey Jack cheese
200g soured cream
200g baby spinach
300g bottled artichokes
grating of nutmeg to taste
400g corn tortillas

1. Combine the cream cheese, 100g of the grated Parmesan, the Monterey Jack cheese and soured cream in a saucepan. Chop the baby spinach and artichokes and mix in with the cheese. Add nutmeg and salt to taste.

2. Preheat the grill. Heat the mixture in a saucepan over a medium heat so it melts. Pour into an ovenproof bowl, sprinkle with the remaining Parmesan, place under the grill until golden brown and bubbling.

3. To make fresh corn chips, cut the tortillas into quarters and deep fry in hot oil. Alternatively you can buy ready-made corn tortillas.

4. Serve the hot fondue with the corn tortilla chips.

Smoked chicken, mango and red chilli tacos

This is a taco with attitude, a global cross-cultural explosion of flavours that takes smoked chicken on a roller-coaster ride of citrus, chilli and coriander flavours. Sit back and pour yourself a glass of cool lemonade, sunshine in your hand and if you are lucky, on your back.

250ml mayonnaise
$^1/_2$ teaspoon each ground cumin and coriander
2 tablespoons coriander, chopped
1 tablespoon chipotle chillies, chopped
juice of 1 lime
400g smoked chicken, cut into strips
1 cos lettuce, trimmed and shredded
$^1/_2$ a red onion, peeled and finely sliced
4 plum tomatoes, quartered and deseeded
3 tablespoons olive oil
1 ripe mango, peeled and cut into strips
8 x 10cm corn or flour tortillas
1 tablespoon jalapeño chillies, chopped
salt and pepper

1. Preheat the grill or griddle pan.

2. Combine the first five ingredients. Season the chicken with salt and pepper and combine.

3. Mix the lettuce, red onion and tomato together, season with salt and pepper and toss with the olive oil.

4. Grill the tortillas.

5. Place the salad in the middle of the tortillas, spoon over the chicken mix and top with the mango strips. Fold in half, sprinkle over the chopped jalapeño and serve.

Tall tales

We took the photograph for this on an early summer's day. Breaking for lunch immediately afterwards was the natural next step, and lasted all of five minutes before the crew had eaten the lot.

3

A fresh look at the world of salads

We love salads. All that
colour and freshness, health and
goodness. You can build them up or down
depending on the occasion, alter a few ingredients or
dressings for added variety. What can go wrong?

The truth is quite a lot. A salad looks easy, it's supposed to.
Orchestrated chaos is one way to describe a salad and if you look
at the one on page 64 you'll see what we mean. What at first appears
random is quickly revealed to be carefully composed.

We think the Americans are the ones to follow when it comes to salad.
They do big ones for lunch, often have them to accompany other things
and regularly start proceedings off with a salad.

There is good reason for this. All that colour provides a
visual feast and with a bit of dressing and seasoning
you get a rewarding plateful of deliciousness.

ALL RECIPES SERVE 4.

Grilled salmon tostada salad

This dish has summer sunshine written all over it; lots of herbs and some citrus notes to kick things into zing territory. If giraffes could dance this might be their reaction. Whether you roll everything up and eat it with your fingers or approach it with a knife and fork is really up to you. We do both, depending on mood and company.

3 tablespoons fresh lime juice
juice of 1 orange
3 tablespoons olive oil
salt and pepper
4 180g salmon fillets
4 flour tortillas

bunch flat-leaf parsley
bunch fresh coriander
bunch mint
1 avocado, stoned, peeled and
chopped
4 vine tomatoes, sliced
1/2 a cucumber, deseeded,
peeled and cut into 1cm cubes
1 small red onion, peeled and
chopped
1 red pepper, trimmed and cut
into 1cm cubes
1 head romaine lettuce,
trimmed of stem end torn
salt and pepper

*Toss the herbs with the avocado,
vine tomatoes, cucumber,
red onion, pepper and lettuce
and add the tequila and lime
dressing. Toss everything
together and check seasoning.*

tomato and mint relish
4 large vine tomatoes
1 small red onion, peeled and
finely chopped
1 jalapeño pepper, trimmed and
finely chopped
2 tablespoons white balsamic
vinegar
bunch freshly chopped mint
2 tablespoons olive oil
salt and pepper

*Combine all the ingredients
and season.*

1. Combine the lime and orange juices with the olive oil, season with salt and pepper. Marinate the salmon fillets for an hour, tossing occasionally.

2. Preheat the grill.

3. Cook the salmon for five minutes each side or until almost but not quite cooked through.

4. Place the tortillas under the grill for a minute to toast slightly (you may have to do two at a time).

5. Spoon the salad on top of the tortillas. Lay a salmon fillet on top and spoon over some tomato and mint relish.

Tall tales

This dish also works well with chicken or other firm white fish like snapper. Somebody tried it with beef fillet recently and it was so well received the chef in question had to make a second batch.

Herby chicken, spiced prawn and mango salad

The combination of chicken and prawns is very popular in Asia where the two proteins are often seen together in dishes as diverse as noodle stir-fries and soups. This is a salad in the same mould, bursting with lots of bold flavours and textures.

2 chicken breasts
2 tablespoons olive oil
2 teaspoons lemon juice
2 tablespoons chopped fresh herbs -
   parsley, thyme, rosemary, tarragon
32 prawns
2 tablespoons peri peri sauce
   (see page 93)
80g pecan nuts
1 mango, peeled and diced
1 cucumber, deseeded and chopped
2 heads little gem lettuce
4 handfuls rocket
salt and pepper

tequila and lime dressing
4 tablespoons mayonnaise
1 tablespoon of coriander, chopped
1 teaspoon of garlic puree
1 lime juiced
1 teaspoon of jalapeños, chopped
1 teaspoon Mexican seasoning
splash of tequila
300ml water
salt and pepper

Mix all ingredients together

1. Season the chicken breasts and combine with the olive oil, lemon juice and herbs. Ensure the chicken is well coated and set aside.

2. Toss the prawns in the peri peri sauce, season with salt and pepper and set aside.

3. Heat a dry frying pan. When hot add the pecans, toss lightly so they toast through for a few minutes and then allow to cool on a plate.

4. Grill or fry the chicken for five minutes either side or until cooked. Grill the prawns for two minutes each side.

5. Slice the chicken. Combine all the salad ingredients, season with salt and pepper and toss with the dressing. Add the chicken, prawns, pecans and mango, toss lightly and serve.

Vietnamese chicken and prawn salad

Cold noodle salads are remarkably refreshing. You need the addition of herbs to make things sing but cold noodles are surprisingly delicious.

250g vermicelli noodles
2 chicken breasts
300g of shelled tiger prawns
200g Chinese cabbage, shredded
100g sugarsnap peas, sliced
1 red pepper, deseeded and sliced
1 green pepper, deseeded and sliced
1 yellow pepper, deseeded and sliced
1 carrot, cut into thin strips
100g rocket leaves
100ml Thai salad dressing
   (see page 33)
25g mint leaves

1. Cook the noodles according to the instructions on the packet.

2. Season and grill or poach the chicken and prawns. Slice the chicken into bite-sized pieces.

3. Combine all the vegetables and rocket leaves with the vermicelli noodles and add the Thai dressing.

4. Mix in the chicken and prawns, check seasoning and pile neatly on to four plates. Sprinkle over the mint leaves.

Tall tales

To get the fragrance from mint leaves slap them with the palm of your hand. This helps to release the flavour.

Thai beef and mint salad

One of the attractions of Eastern food is the inventive use of vegetables. This is a warm salad, an Eastern equivalent to those French salads you find in lunchtime bistros with sautéed chicken livers, lots of leaves and meat juices acting as the dressing.

2 sirloin steaks, each weighing
  around 180g
1 tablespoon light soy sauce
1 tablespoon mirin
2 green chillies, finely sliced
2 tablespoons fresh lime juice
3 tablespoons vegetable oil
2 cloves garlic, peeled and crushed
1 tablespoon fish sauce
1 tablespoon brown sugar
2 Lebanese cucumbers, thinly sliced
1 red onion, peeled and thinly sliced
2 little gem lettuces, trimmed
2 tablespoons mint leaves, roughly
  chopped
1 tablespoon sweet basil leaves
salt and pepper

1. Combine the beef with the soy sauce, mirin, chillies and lime juice for 30 minutes, or overnight in the fridge for best results.

2. Heat a frying pan or wok, add the oil and cook the beef for three to four minutes, or until just colouring. Add the garlic, fish sauce and sugar and simmer for another two minutes. Set aside and rest for five mins, then slice into half-centimetre slices.

3. Combine the cucumber, red onion and lettuce with the mint and basil. Season with salt and pepper and toss well. Divide onto four plates. Lay the beef slices on top and serve. The sauce from the beef will form the dressing.

Tall tales

A Lebanese cucumber? What are they? They are shorter than your average cucumber and are dryer and consequently meatier. They still taste similar, just with a bit more attitude. Can't find them? Don't worry, a cucumber will do fine.

Sushi brown rice salad with smoked salmon

We are big fans of sushi; all those healthy ingredients served on a rice boat. What, we wondered, would happen if we took the idea but got rid of the boat. Or rather deconstructed it. Messed it up a bit. Well, this is where we got to – a healthy combination of raw ingredients given an Eastern twist with a spiky dressing.

200g brown basmati rice
1 teaspoon wasabi
1 tablespoon soy
1 tablespoon mirin
3cm piece ginger, peeled and grated
4 handfuls baby spinach
1 white radish (mouli), cut into thin strips
1 cucumber, deseeded and cut into diamonds
1 avocado, destoned and diced
2 carrots, cut into thin strips
salt and pepper
280g smoked salmon
1 tablespoon each sesame and black onion seeds
4 sheets nori seaweed
4 spring onions, finely sliced on the diagonal
2 limes, halved

1. Cook the rice in plenty of salted water until tender. Drain and refresh in cold water.

2. Whisk the wasabi, soy, mirin and ginger together to make a dressing.

3. Toss with the rice, spinach, white radish , cucumber, avocado and carrot. Season. Lay a sheet of nori on each plate and pile the salad neatly on top. Dot the salmon among the leaves.

4. Heat a dry frying pan over a moderate heat and when hot add the seeds, toast briefly, 15-20 seconds should be sufficient.

5. Scatter over the seeds and spring onions and serve with a lime wedge.

Bang bang chicken salad

Chicken, lots of fresh vegetables and herbs and some slippery succulent noodles is all it takes for this easy-to-make and very delicious salad. The trick is in the tossing. The ingredients need to get to know each other rather well. A scant tossing means no real connection, so toss vigorously to create some chemistry.

2 chicken breasts
1 tablespoon soy sauce
1 tablespoon sesame oil
1 tablespoon fish sauce
1 chilli, trimmed and finely chopped
400g egg noodles
1 tablespoon olive oil
120g beanshoots
2 carrots, julienned
2 red chillies, julienned
1/2 a cucumber, halved, deseeded and
    sliced
1 head romaine lettuce, trimmed and
    shredded
1 tablespoon picked mint leaves
2 tablespoons peanuts
2 handfuls Chinese leaves, shredded
2 tablespoons satay dipping sauce
salt and pepper

1. Cover the chicken breasts loosely in clingfilm and bash with a rolling pin to half their original thickness. Combine with the next four ingredients and toss well. Set aside.

2. Cook the noodles according to the instructions on the packet. Drain and refresh in cold water.

3. Lightly oil and season the chicken breasts and barbecue or fry for three to four minutes each, or until cooked. Allow to rest for five minutes and cut into strips.

4. Combine the noodles with the other ingredients, add the chicken, season with salt and pepper and toss well.

Our style chicken Waldorf salad with dried cranberries and pecans

What makes a Waldorf salad? Some say walnuts, others celery, others say it's a combination of these ingredients and more. It was supposed to have been first served in the Waldorf Astoria Hotel in New York, so we have taken the American theme and adapted it somewhat (we are not that keen on mayonnaise for this dish, for example).

$^1/_2$ tablespoon grain mustard
$^1/_2$ tablespoon Dijon mustard
$^1/_2$ tablespoon honey
4 tablespoons white wine vinegar
100ml olive oil
$^1/_2$ a lemon, juiced
salt and pepper

2 chicken breasts, cut into thin strips
1 pear, peeled and sliced
1 apple, peeled and sliced
2 sticks celery, washed and cut into
    thin strips
1 head chicory, leaves separated
60g pecans, roughly chopped
80g dried cranberries, soaked in warm
    water for 10 minutes or until soft
4 handfuls watercress
4 radishes, sliced

1. Combine all the ingredients for the dressing in a jam jar and shake well.

2. Place the dressing in the bowl. Heat a frying pan and when hot, fry the chicken in a scant tablespoon of olive oil and a seasoning of salt and pepper. Cook for five minutes or until coloured and cooked through. Transfer to the bowl with the dressing and toss lightly.

3. Combine the remaining ingredients in a bowl and add the chicken and dressing. Mix everything together and season well.

4. Serve on individual plates or in a large bowl in the centre of the table.

Tall tales

Try the same treatment with tuna. Both also work well as a sandwich. We prefer it open, its a height thing, but closed is also good. In a soft bun is even better.

Roast duck, watercress and orange salad

We have always rather liked the idea of duck a l'orange, but too often it is sickly sweet and a massive disappointment. However, the idea is very attractive, so we started to look at how we might take the ingredients and put them together in a fresh, light, modern way. This is the result.

4 tablespoons light soy sauce
2 tablespoons honey
2 tablespoons olive oil
4 duck breasts
1 teaspoon fresh lemon juice
2 tablespoons balsamic vinegar
1 tablespoon Dijon mustard
1 garlic clove, peeled, chopped and
    mashed with a little salt
6 tablespoons olive oil
2 oranges
handful of radicchio, shredded
bunch of watercress
1 small red onion, peeled and finely
    chopped
salt and pepper

1. Whisk two tablespoons of soy sauce, the honey and olive oil together in a shallow bowl. Add the duck breasts and leave for two hours, tossing occasionally.

2. Whisk the remaining soy, lemon juice, balsamic vinegar, mustard and garlic together, season with salt and pepper and whisk in the olive oil.

3. Trim the top and bottom of the oranges, cut off skin so there is no pith and cut the orange into segments. Set aside.

4. Toss the radicchio and watercress together with the red onion.

5. Heat a frying pan over a moderate heat for five minutes. Season the duck and place, skin side down, in the hot pan for four minutes. Turn over and repeat. This will leave the duck pink. If you want it more well done leave for another couple of minutes on each side.

6. Let the duck rest for at least five minutes and slice diagonally.

7. Toss the watercress and radicchio mixture with the orange segments, dressing and duck. Check seasoning and serve.

Tall tales

Blood orange makes for a seasonal change around February and March. Grapefruit, too, combines wonderfully with duck.

Healthy feta salad

Lots of fresh vegetables, a little cheese for protein and our infamous house dressing. This is a summer salad with crunch, attitude and colour.

200g feta cheese, sliced
1 teaspoon fresh oregano leaves
olive oil
200g broccoli, broken into florets
500g quinoa
100g sugar snaps
1 400g tin borlotti beans, well rinsed
    and drained
1 avocado, destoned and diced
4 handfuls rocket, washed
2 handfuls baby spinach
1 punnet cherry tomatoes, halved
4 tablespoons herby house dressing
1 tablespoon mixed toasted pumpkin
    and sesame seeds

herby house dressing
1 tablespoon fresh basil, chopped
1 teaspoon fresh oregano, chopped
1 teaspoon fresh tarragon, chopped
4 tablespoons olive oil
1 teaspoon Dijon mustard
1 tablespoon white wine vinegar
salt and pepper

Whisk all ingredients together

1. Combine the feta cheese with the oregano, a few grinds of black pepper and enough olive oil to cover. This will keep for several days in the fridge.

2. Blanch the broccoli in plenty of salted water for three minutes or until tender. Drain and refresh under cold water. Cook the quinoa according to the instructions on the packet.

3. Toss the broccoli with the quinoa, vegetables, herby house dressing and a seasoning of salt and pepper. Scatter over the cherry tomatoes, feta and toasted seeds and check seasoning.

Tall tales

You can marinade firm goat's cheese in olive oil like this. Chilli makes a welcome addition, garlic too.

Grilled tuna and Provençal salad

They may not have giraffes in Provence, but every giraffe has a little of Provence within them. For some it is the sunshine, for others the vibrant, revealing colours. In all its the laid-back summertime feeling. Think lavender and honey, olive oil and fantastic vegetables. This is Provence on a plate.

1 tablespoon capers, well rinsed
2 garlic cloves, peeled and finely chopped
bunch basil, roughly chopped
large handful of spinach
bunch parsley, roughly chopped
1 teaspoon Dijon mustard
2 tablespoons white wine vinegar
6 tablespoons olive oil plus a little extra for coating the tuna and for serving

4 eggs
8 baby plum tomatoes, halved
1 red onion, peeled and sliced
1 bulb fennel, trimmed and thinly sliced
1 400g tin artichokes
1 400g tin cannellini beans
100g pitted black olives
2 heads chicory, trimmed

4 tuna steaks, each weighing about 160g
1 lemon, quartered

1. Blitz the first eight ingredients in a liquidiser to form a paste. If it is too thick add a little water.

2. Cook the eggs in boiling water for four and a half minutes, drain and cool under cold running water. Peel and set aside.

3. Toss the remaining ingredients with the dressing and divide on to four plates. Season and lightly oil the tuna and cook on a hot grill for one minute each side. Serve on top of the salad along with the eggs, halved. Drizzle over some olive oil and serve with a lemon wedge.

Tall tales

Tuna is something of a political fish, given stocks of certain species are somewhat depleted. At Giraffe we source sustainable yellow-fin tuna. After all, what is the point in stripping the oceans?

Warm bacon, blue cheese, mango and avocado salad

The classic blue cheese salad is very French and delicious it is too. But we are known to play around with things a bit so this version has been Giraffed with some added crunch and zing. Which blue cheese you use is up to you. We are rather fond of Cashel Blue, it's an Irish cheese, but there are many to choose from and all work well.

6 slices streaky bacon

$^1/_2$ ciabatta

4 tablespoons olive oil, plus extra for the croutons

juice of 1 lemon

1 tablespoon red wine vinegar

1 teaspoon honey

1 garlic clove, peeled and crushed

1 small red onion, peeled and sliced

225g blue cheese

2 mangoes, peeled and diced

2 avocados, peeled and diced

1 tablespoon toasted pumpkin seeds

1 head romaine lettuce, separated and stem ends removed

bunch coriander leaves

bunch flat leaf parsley

1 teaspoon oregano leaves

1. Grill the bacon until crispy, drain on kitchen paper and break into bite-sized pieces.

2. Cut the ciabatta into 2cm cubes, toss with a little olive oil and grill until golden and crispy, about five or six minutes but you need to turn them a couple of times.

3. Whisk the lemon juice, red wine vinegar, honey and garlic. Drizzle in the olive oil, whisking all the time and then add the red onion.

4. Combine the remaining ingredients in a salad bowl and season with salt and pepper.

5. Pour over the dressing and toss with the bacon and croutons. Check seasoning and serve.

Tall tales

Toasting nuts and seeds is best done in a dry frying pan over a moderate heat. Wait for the pan to get hot and then watch things carefully, the toasting happens quicker than a giraffe might nibble its way through a leaf.

Powerfood salad bowl

This is a bright, full-flavoured salad that lets the vegetables do the talking. Ring the changes by varying the spice mix on the squash or by choosing different vegetables; cauliflower works well, as does asparagus when the latter is in its short, early summer season.

1 small butternut squash, peeled and cut into chunks
1 teaspoon each ground cumin and coriander
2 tablespoons vegetable oil
salt and pepper
1 large head broccoli
100g French beans
4 tablespoons herby house dressing (see page 64)
1 tablespoon cashew nuts, roughly chopped dry roasted
2 tablespoons (defrosted) edamame beans or muki beans
2 cooked beetroot, diced
4 handfuls mixed salad leaves
2 handfuls baby spinach
1 tablespoon sunflower seeds
1 tablespoon pumpkin seeds

1. Preheat the oven to 180C/gas mark 4.

2. Toss the squash with the spices, oil and a seasoning of salt and pepper. Roast in the oven for 20 minutes or until tender. Set aside to cool.

3. Cut the broccoli into bite-size pieces. Cut the beans in half. Blanch together in salted boiling water for three to four minutes or until cooked but still crunchy. Drain in cold water and while still warm toss in the dressing.

4. Add the squash to the beans and broccoli along with the nuts, edamame, beetroot, salad leaves and spinach. Season as you go.

5. Place a frying pan on a moderate heat and when hot add the sunflower and pumpkin seeds. Cook, tossing occasionally, for a couple of minutes or until just lightly coloured.

6. Scatter the seeds over the salad and serve.

Tall tales

Come the autumn there are other squashes to choose from, but we find the butternut the most consistently delicious of them all. Butternut also makes a stunning soup and an extremely good risotto.

4

Easy stir-fries, curries and noodle bowls

Meal in a bowl, street
food, easy food. Noodles are just
so perfect for our busy modern lives. Fresh,
healthy food served up fast. What is there not to like?
Low protein counts and lots of vegetables tick so many
boxes. And when things are as delicious as this...

The secret to success when cooking in a wok is all in the preparation
— chopping before you start cooking. Little bowls help to keep things
organised. The mantra is to cook then season. And taste as you go.

If you are new to this kind of cooking you'll need to invest in a
few items like soy sauce and teriyaki. But don't worry,
they keep for ages.

As a rule, Asian stores are a better place to
shop. Not only do you get the specialist
herbs more easily, they come
in bigger bunches. And more
attitude. The herbs that is.

ALL RECIPES SERVE 4.

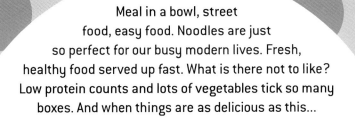

Firecracker sesame chicken and egg noodle stir-fry

Mix and matching is very Giraffe. Just don't call it fusion. Fantastic noodles, crunchy chicken. Delicious. An Eastern-inspired promise delivered. Quick, simple and easy. Don't skimp on the coriander, it is all-important.

5 tablespoons breadcrumbs
4 tablespoons coriander, chopped
1 tablespoon mixed sesame seeds
2 teaspoons Japanese chilli pepper
4 chicken breasts
plain flour
salt and pepper
1 egg beaten with two tablespoons milk

600g egg or hokkien noodles
4 tablespoons vegetable oil
1 red pepper, deseeded and sliced
150g shitake mushrooms, sliced
1 red onion, peeled and sliced
$^1/_2$ teaspoon each grated ginger, five spice powder and chopped red chilli
100g sugarsnap peas
2 heads bok choi
$^1/_2$ Chinese cabbage, cut into 2cm slices
100ml dark soy sauce
100ml sweet chilli sauce
1 tablespoon toasted sesame seed oil
1 tablespoon toasted sesame seeds
2 limes halved

1. Combine the breadcrumbs, coriander, sesame seeds and chilli powder.

2. Cover each chicken breast with a sheet of clingfilm and bash with a rolling pin to flatten so each breast is about a centimetre thick.

3. Season two tablespoons of flour with salt and pepper. Dip the chicken breasts in the seasoned flour, then in the egg mixture, then in the breadcrumb mixture.

egg noddle stir-fry

1. Cook the noodles according to the instructions on the packet, drain and refresh under cold water. Set aside.

2. Heat the vegetable oil in a wok and stir fry the peppers, mushrooms and red onion for two minutes. Add the ginger, five spice and chilli and cook for two further minutes. Add the peas, bok choi and Chinese cabbage and cook for two more minutes.

3. Slice the chicken into strips and add to the wok along with the noodles, toss so everything is heated through and finish off with the soy and chilli sauces. Divide on to four plates, sprinkle over the sesame oil and seeds and garnish with a lime half on each plate.

4. You can also serve this dish with pineapple salsa, which is a somewhat lighter approach.

pineapple salsa

Quarter pineapple cut into 1cm cubes

1 green chilli, trimmed and finely
chopped

1 spring onion, finely sliced including
the green part

small bunch fresh coriander, roughly
chopped

1/2 cucumber, deseeded and finely
diced

1 tablespoon olive oil

juice of 2 limes

salt and pepper

1 tablespoon soy sauce

1 tablespoon rice vinegar

*Combine all the ingredients, mix well
and serve with the chicken*

Easy Thai green chicken curry with organic brown rice

Curry is easy to make. A stew with spices really. But a good curry with zing, zest and attitude is another thing entirely. Authenticity matters slightly less to us than capturing a freshness and vitality. The brown rice is just a little more healthy than white, but it's the nutty, wholesome flavour which works with the curry that we really like.

200g organic brown rice
100g sugarsnap peas
3 tablespoons vegetable oil
100g butternut squash, cut into 2cm dice
1 tablespoon Thai green curry paste
4 fresh kaffir lime leaves
500g chicken breast, cut into strips
2 teaspoons palm sugar, or dark brown sugar
200ml chicken stock
400ml can coconut cream
1 tablespoon Thai fish sauce
4 tablespoons coriander, finely chopped

1. Soak the rice in cold water.

2. Blanch the sugarsnap peas in boiling salted water for three minutes, drain and refresh under cold water.

3. Heat two tablespoons of the oil in a wok or large pan and sauté the squash for eight to 10 minutes or until lightly coloured. Set aside.

4. Heat a further tablespoon of oil in the wok and add the curry paste and lime leaves and fry over a medium heat for one or two minutes. Add the chicken and palm sugar and cook for two to three minutes, then add the stock and coconut cream and cook for a further 12-15 minutes until the chicken is cooked and the sauce slightly reduced.

5. Drain the rice, bring a saucepan of lightly salted water to the boil, add the rice and cook for eight to 10 minutes or until tender.

6. Add the fish sauce to the curry along with the chopped coriander and finally add the peas and squash.

7. Serve with the rice.

Tall tales

Pumpkin comes in many shapes and forms and size varies enormously. We find butternut squash the most consistent both in terms of texture and flavour. As a rough rule however, size seems to us giraffes to run in direct conflict with taste. It's a rare occasion for a giraffe to say stay small but this is definitely one of them.

Black pepper stir-fry with chilli tomato jam

Simple, quick and easy, this stir-fry relies on a few store-cupboard staples and the freshest of ingredients for its flavour.

chilli and tomato jam
500ml thai sweet chilli sauce
3 beef tomatoes, quartered, seeded and diced (or 1/2 a tin of chopped tomatoes)
1 red onion, finely diced

500g udon noodles
4 tablespoons vegetable oil
1 red pepper, deseeded and sliced thinly
150g shitake mushrooms, stems removed and sliced
1 sliced red onion, peeled and sliced
350g timed rump steak, cut into strips
1/2 tablespoons grated ginger
1/2 tablespoons red chillis, chopped
2 heads bok choi, roughly chopped
1/2 Chinese cabbage, sliced
2 tablespoons dark sesame oil
100ml dark soy sauce
100ml thai sweet chilli sauce

1. Combine the ingredients for the sweet chilli jam in a small saucepan. Simmer over a low heat for 10 minutes or until syrupy.

2. Cook the noodles according to the instructions on the packet, drain, refresh under cold water and set aside.

3. Heat the vegetable oil in a wok over a high heat and stir-fry the peppers, mushrooms and red onion for two minutes or until coloured. Add the beef, ginger and chilli, wok for two minues and then add the bok choi and Chinese cabbage. Wok so everything cooks and is well combined.

4. Add the sesame oil, soy and sweet chilli sauce, toss to combine and check seasoning.

5. Serve with a dollop of sweet chilli jam on the side.

Tall tales

Sesame oil has quite a low burning point which is why you add it towards the end of cooking. Its inclusion is part flavour, part texture, adding a rich exotic touch.

Udon noodles are traditionally served up in a soup made of a light broth and topped with thinly sliced spring onions. We rather like them in stir-fries, their unctuous quality allows for slurping of the best kind which is just what noodle eating should be about.

Other things to do with udon noodles:
Combine with a chicken broth, sliced spring onions and bok choi with a splash of soy
Serve cold with a sweet chilli dipping sauce – this is very Japanese
If you cant get udon noodles or fancy a change then try soba noodles which are equally yummy

Sweet basil and chilli-prawn stir-fry

The simplicity of stir-fries is undoubtedly part of their attraction. You chop, you cook, you eat. But getting depth of flavour into a stir-fry can be a challenge. A giraffe nibbles away but some nibbles are decidedly better than others. The two-stage approach of this dish means the sauce is flavoured with the prawns before everything comes together and is enlivened with the basil. Deep and fresh doesn't exactly trip off the tongue but you get our drift…

chilli prawn sauce
400g raw prawns, shelled
vegetable oil
1 red chilli, trimmed and finely
    chopped
3 garlic cloves, finely chopped
2 tablespoons fresh ginger, grated
1 small onion, peeled and chopped
1 400g tin chopped tomatoes
salt and pepper

500g udon or egg noodles
1 red onion, peeled and sliced
1 red pepper, deseeded and sliced
    lengthways
150g shitake mushrooms, sliced
1/2 Chinese cabbage, cut into 1cm
    slices
2 heads bok choi leaves, separated
60g bamboo shoots
60g water chestnuts
3 tablespoons dark soy sauce
1 tablespoon Thai basil, chopped
3 spring onions, sliced
2 limes, halved

1. For the sauce, fry the prawns in two tablespoons of oil over a medium heat for three minutes or until coloured. Remove and set aside. Add the chilli, garlic and ginger, fry for two minutes. Add the onion and fry for three minutes or until starting to colour. Add the tomatoes, season with salt and pepper and cook for five minutes. Check seasoning.

2. Cook the noodles according to the instructions on the packet, drain, refresh under cold water and set aside.

3. Heat four tablespoons of vegetable oil in a wok and stir-fry the red onion, pepper and mushrooms for three minutes. Add the Chinese cabbage, bok choi, bamboo shoots and water chestnuts and continue cooking for two minutes. Add the soy sauce, noodles and chilli sauce and continue cooking so everything is heated through.

4. Return the prawns to the wok, mix and scatter over the basil and serve with the spring onions and a wedge of lime.

Tall tales

Thai basil has a very distinctive note – spicy and citrus fresh – something very evocative of the country itself. It can be tricky to find, however, as it needs to be fresh to give off its best flavour. There really isn't a suitable substitute. Some chopped mint and coriander would be entirely different but they would lend a freshness.

Balinese chilli lamb and egg noodle stir-fry

Sambal oelek is often served as a condiment. It's like a fiery hot Tabasco, made with crushed chillies and vinegar. For those who like chilli heat you can serve it on the side – or leave it out altogether – and use fresh chillies instead.

500g neck of lamb, cut into bite-sized strips
1 tablespoon sambal oelek
2 tablespoons light soy sauce
1 tablespoon fish sauce
2 garlic cloves, peeled and finely chopped
1 teaspoon dark brown sugar or palm sugar
400g egg noodles
3 tablespoons vegetable oil
1 tablespoon peanuts, chopped
1 handful French beans, trimmed
1 handful sugar snap peas
150ml beef or chicken stock
juice of 1 lime
1 tablespoon mint, finely chopped

1. Combine the lamb with the sambal oelek, soy and fish sauces, garlic and sugar and leave aside for 30 minutes.

2. Cook the noodles according to the instructions on the packet, drain and refresh in cold water.

3. Heat the oil in a wok and cook over a moderate heat, stir-fry the nuts until golden brown and remove. Add the lamb and French beans, cook for two minutes and then add the sugar snaps and cook for a further two to three minutes. Add the stock and lime juice and cook until the meat is tender, for a futher three to four minutes.

4. Fold in the noodles, coat in the sauce and season with mint.

Hot Thai duck noodle stir-fry with chilli jam

Duck is fantastic with all these Asian flavours. Rich and succulent, the soy and ginger cut right through the meat.

400g egg noodles
4 tablespoons vegetable oil
1 tablespoon ginger and chilli paste
1 red onion, peeled and sliced
1 red pepper, deseeded and sliced lengthways
150g shitake mushrooms, sliced
4 bok choi, washed and cut in half lengthways
400g cooked duck meat
2 tablespoons teriyaki sauce
few sprigs Thai holy basil, finely shredded
few sprigs mint, finely shredded
chilli jam (see page 75)
crispy shallots to garnish (see page 80)
few sprigs coriander

1. Cook the noodles according to the instructions on the packet. Drain, refresh with cold water and set aside.

2. Heat wok or non-stick frying pan over a medium heat. Add the oil and chilli paste and infuse for five seconds. Add all the vegetables and stir-fry for one minute.

3. Add the duck and continue cooking until the duck is heated through. Add the noodles and toss through evenly. Add the teriyaki sauce and cook for a further 30 seconds.

4. Remove from the heat and add the shredded mint and Thai basil.

5. Pile up as high as you can on four plates. Top with the chilli jam and garnish with crispy shallots and coriander.

Tall tales

Ginger and chilli paste is somewhat more than the sum of its parts. A surprisingly meaty mouthful tempered with the zing of ginger. If you are chilli averse just be a bit sparing but don't leave it out altogether or you'll risk losing the soul of the dish.

Phod Malay udon noodle stir-fry

There is a tendency for vegetarian food to focus on protein in the form of dairy or egg. Occasionally, however, it seems a welcome change to have a vegetable dish that is, well, vegetables. This dish has a mild Asian flavour but no real chilli kick.

6 tablespoons vegetable oil

4 tablespoons shallots, finely sliced

1 red onion, peeled and sliced

1 red pepper, deseeded and sliced lengthways

150g shitake mushrooms, sliced

2 handfuls sugarsnap peas, halved lengthways

2 handfuls beansprouts

2 bok choi, trimmed and quartered lengthways

500g udon noodles, cooked according to the instructions on the packet

1 tablespoon teriyaki sauce

phod malay paste

1 tablespoon vegetable oil

1 white onion, diced

1 teaspoon ground coriander

1 teaspoon ground cumin

1 teaspoon turmeric

1 teaspoon thai red curry paste

2 tablespoon tomato paste

$1/2$ cup roasted peanuts, finely crushed

$1/2$ cup of water

1 tablespoon sesame oil

Sweat onions and spices until soft. Add curry, tomato paste, and water and cook for 5 min. Cool down and blitz. Add the sesame oil.

1. Heat the vegetable oil over a medium heat. Add half the shallots and cook slowly until golden brown. Remove with a slotted spoon on to kitchen paper and repeat with the second half. If you try to do all the shallots in one go they will burn.

2. Heat a wok or large frying pan over a moderate heat and when nice and hot add four tablespoons vegetable oil. Add the red onion, pepper, mushrooms, sugarsnaps, beansprouts and bok choi and stir-fry for two to three minutes.

3. Add the udon noodles and continue to stir-fry. Add the malay paste, teriyaki sauce and a little water, about two tablespoons, to make a sauce. Toss so everything is well coated and serve with the crispy shallots on top.

Giraffe-style lamb rogan josh

Global hopping is a hallmark of Giraffe. We stick our necks out from Mexico to Malaysia and pretty much everywhere in between, but India is a country we are only just starting to explore. Rogan Josh is something of a national dish, if you can have such a thing in what is such a huge country with so many regional influences. This is our version.

2 teaspoons cumin
2 teaspoons ground cardamom
2 teaspoons sweet paprika
3cm piece of ginger, crushed
$1/2$ teaspoon cayenne pepper, or
    to taste
juice of 1 lemon
1kg leg of lamb, diced
25g butter
4 tablespoons vegetable oil
2 small onions, sliced
2 garlic cloves, peeled and finely
    chopped
1 tin chopped tomatoes
150ml chicken stock
3 bay leaves
2 cinnamon sticks
bunch fresh coriander
100g toasted almonds, chopped
1 red chilli, finely sliced
250g yoghurt

1. Combine the cumin, cardamom, paprika, ginger, cayenne pepper and lemon juice. Toss with the lamb. If you can leave this to marinate so much the better.

2. Heat the butter and oil in a large frying pan over a moderate heat. Colour the meat in batches. Add the onion, fry for five minutes or until lightly coloured, add the garlic, then the tomatoes, stock, bay leaves and cinnamon sticks. Bring to the boil, return the lamb and simmer for one hour or until the lamb is tender – make sure you keep enough liquid in there and don't leave to dry out. Stir in the fresh coriander.

3. Scatter over the almonds and fresh chilli and serve with the yoghurt.

5

Main
plates

What makes a plate main? Size matters, a bit. But for us it's a little more complicated than that. We like colour, it makes us smile. And we like a contrast in textures.

Protein is important, but not overly so. You can have too much of a good thing. You'll see we are rather keen on chicken. It's versatile, easy to eat and has universal appeal among all age groups.

We are also pretty enthusiastic about vegetables. Not only do they bring colour, but lots of crunch appeal. People often say they don't like vegetables, but we see this as a challenge.

Starch is also important; we like bread and potatoes, but pasta and rice are also cool. So we do lots of mixing and matching.

Colour, variety and texture make things more attractive. Clean plates you might say.

ALL RECIPES SERVE 4.

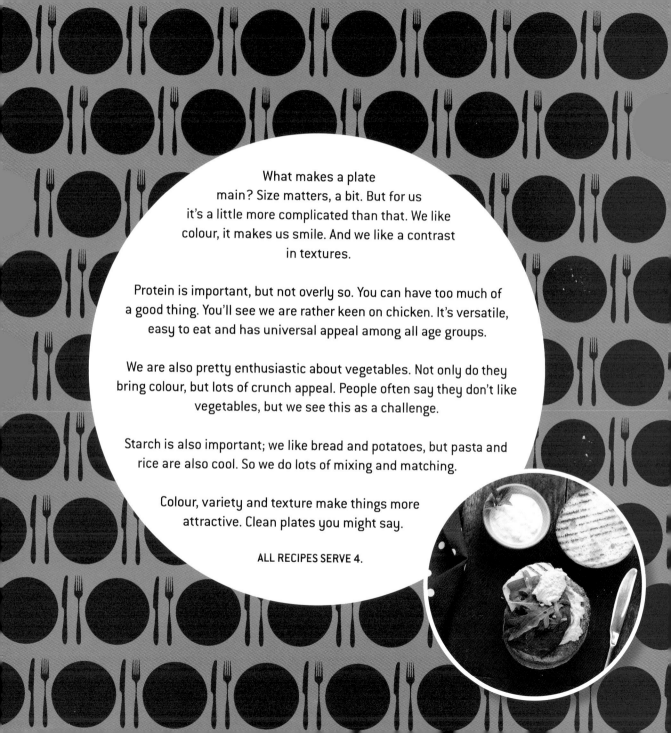

Lamb satay with napa cabbage and green onion slaw

Grilled meats and salads are the mainstay of so many barbecues and with good reason. Chargrilled meat balanced with fresh and crunchy salads. It's a ying and yang thing, something we subscribe to big time. Mayonnaise has its place, but this slaw is all about fresh, vibrant flavours. Health in a bowl.

800g lamb fillet, cut into 3cm pieces
1 red onion, cut into 3cm dice
4 sticks of lemongrass, tough outer leaves removed

lamb marinade
80ml soy sauce
1 tablespoon soft brown sugar
1 tablespoon coriander, finely chopped
pinch turmeric
40ml sesame oil

spicy peanut sauce
$^1/_2$ tablespoon thai red curry paste
2 tablespoons vegetable oil
270ml coconut milk
40ml soy sauce
200g crunchy peanut butter
50ml sweet chilli sauce
1 tablespoon lime juice
1 tablespoon mint, chopped

napa cabbage and green onion slaw
$^1/_2$ napa or Chinese cabbage, shredded
2 carrots, cut into thin strips
4 spring onions, sliced
1 red chilli, finely sliced
1 red onion, thinly sliced
100ml dark soy sauce
2 tablespoons sweet chilli sauce
2 tablespoons toasted sesame oil
2 tablespoons roasted peanuts, crushed
2 tablespoons rice wine vinegar
4 handfuls washed baby spinach
juice of one lime
salt and pepper

1. Skewer the lamb and red onion onto the lemongrass.

2. Combine the marinade ingredients and toss the skewers in the mixture. Set aside for one hour, or overnight in the fridge.

3. Preheat the grill or chargrill and cook the skewers for eight to 10 minutes, turning occasionally, until done. Remove and allow to rest for five minutes.

4. Cook the curry paste in the oil, in a wok or frying pan, for three to four minutes or until it loses its raw aroma. Add the coconut milk, soy sauce, peanut butter and sweet chilli sauce, and bring to the boil. Simmer for three minutes, remove from the heat and stir in the lime juice and mint.

5. Combine all the ingredients for the slaw, toss well and check seasoning.

6. Serve the skewers on top of the slaw with a little of the sauce on the side.

Sunday night mac and cheese
...with a little bit of jerk spice and roast chicken

Mac and cheese has become something of a fashionable dish, launched or relaunched on to the scene when restaurants finally woke up to the idea that inexpensive comfort eating was something people wanted at least some of the time. This is a cheap dish and easy to prepare, but its real attraction lies in that homely combination of pasta and chicken, a really simple Sunday supper.

1 litre milk
250ml double cream
1 onion, peeled and roughly chopped
2 garlic cloves, crushed
200g butter
80g plain flour
bunch flat-leaf parsley, finely chopped
1 teaspoon fresh oregano, picked
1 teaspoon fresh thyme leaves
1 tablespoon fresh sage, finely chopped
salt and pepper
2 teaspoons mustard
600g aged cheddar, grated
200g Parmesan, grated, plus a little extra for the topping
400g penne pasta
300g cooked chicken
1 teaspoon jerk seasoning (see page 114)
panko Japanese breadcrumbs or home-made ones work just as well

1. Combine the milk, cream, onion and garlic in a saucepan, bring to the boil and set aside.

2. In another saucepan melt 100g of butter with the flour, cook for three minutes over a low heat and then pour the milk into the flour mixture slowly. Add the herbs to the sauce and cook for five minutes or until it no long tastes of flour. Season with salt and pepper and stir in the mustard. Remove from the heat and stir in the cheeses.

3. Cook the pasta in plenty of salted water until almost tender. Drain and refresh under cold water.

4. Preheat the oven to 180C/gas mark 4. Butter an ovenproof dish.

5. Toss the chicken with the jerk seasoning. Place the pasta in the dish along with the chicken and pour over the sauce. Scatter over the breadcrumbs and parmesan (about two tablespoons). Dot with the remaining butter. Bake for 25-30 minutes or until brown and bubbling.

6. Serve with a green salad, topped with the chives.

Tall tales

The possible additions are endless but try:
Grilled aubergine and courgette
12 slow-roasted tomatoes with their juices
A light flaked fish, like cod, haddock or hake

Tequila and lime chicken breast on paella fried rice

This dish is a celebration of Mexico in all its colourful glory. Mexican cuisine is much more than the Tex-Mex many of us have been exposed to; while some dishes are spiked generously with chilli the real focus is on balance; bright colours set against good punchy ingredients. If the paella sounds like a step too far, serve the chicken and salsa with wilted spinach or broccoli.

4 chicken breasts, skinned
juice and zest of one lime
2 garlic cloves, peeled and grated
1 red chilli finely chopped
25ml shot of tequila
100ml olive oil
1 teaspoon ground cumin
1 teaspoon paprika
1 tablespoon coriander stems chopped

Combine all the ingredients. Toss gently, cover with clingfilm and refrigerate overnight.

paella fried rice

3 tablespoons vegetable oil
1 red onion, roughly chopped
1 red chilli, finely chopped
1 red pepper, deseeded and finely chopped
1 yellow pepper, deseeded and finely chopped
1 stick celery, finely diced
300g long-grain rice
1 teaspoon ground coriander
1 teaspoon turmeric and paprika

1 teaspoon dried oregano
1 tablespoon tomato puree
300ml chicken stock
1x 800g tin sweetcorn, drained and rinsed
3 beef tomatoes, seeded and diced
2 tablespoons coriander, roughly chopped
2 limes, halved

mango salsa

1 ripe mango, peeled and diced
1 red onion, peeled and chopped
1 red chilli, trimmed and chopped
2 spring onions, sliced
2 garlic cloves, peeled and chopped
1 tablespoon coriander, roughly chopped
150ml olive oil
zest and juice of one lime
1 beef tomato, deseeded and chopped

Combine all the salsa ingredients, season with salt and pepper and refrigerate.

1. Heat the oil in a wok or large frying pan and add the onion, chilli, peppers and celery. Cook for five minutes without colouring. Add the rice, stir so it is well coated in the oil and then add the coriander, turmeric, paprika and oregano. Cook for two minutes and then add the tomato puree, chicken stock and 300ml of water. Bring to the boil and simmer for 15 minutes or until the rice is tender. Add the sweetcorn and diced tomatoes. Remove from the heat and stir in the chopped coriander.

2. In a shallow pan heat three tablespoons of olive oil. Wipe the marinade from the chicken breasts, season and colour for two minutes on one side. Turn over and repeat on the other side. Put the lid on, lower the heat, and cook for 10 minutes or until the chicken is just tender. Allow to rest for five minutes.

3. Serve the chicken on top of the rice with the salsa spooned over the top and a wedge of lime.

Lamb chop tagine with minted fluffy couscous

A tagine is normally made with a less tender cut of lamb and therefore needs long slow-cooking. This is a speedy version, something that really can be whipped up when you get home. Apart from the chops, all these ingredients are in any good store-cupboard and fridge.

8 lamb chops
3 tablespoons olive oil
1 onion, peeled and finely chopped
3 garlic cloves, peeled and finely
    chopped
2 teaspoons ground cumin
1 teaspoon ground ginger
1 teaspoon turmeric
1 teaspoon sweet paprika
$^1/_2$ teaspoon ground cinnamon
600ml beef stock
1 tablespoon tomato puree
1 400g tin chickpeas, well rinsed
    and drained
35g pitted green olives
200g prunes
juice of 1 lemon
2 tablespoons coriander, chopped
salt and pepper

minted fluffy couscous
250g couscous
1 beef tomato, deseeded and diced
Bunch of mint, finely chopped
1 small red onion, peeled and finely
    diced

1. Season and colour the lamb chops in the olive oil until nicely brown, about two minutes each side, and set aside.

2. In the same oil, sauté the onion over a moderate heat for 10 minutes without colouring. Add the garlic and spices and cook for two minutes. Add the beef stock and tomato puree and season with salt and pepper. Simmer over a low heat for 20 minutes.

3. Add the lamb chops, chickpeas, olives and prunes and simmer for another 10 minutes. Add the lemon juice, check seasoning and stir in the coriander.

minty fluffy cous-cous

1. Add an equal quantity of boiling water to the couscous. Leave to stand for five minutes. Fluff up with a fork. Season with salt and pepper and stir in the mint, tomato and red onion.

Tall tales

If you like your couscous toasted add to a hot dry frying pan once rehydrated and cook over a low heat stirring occasionally for 10 minutes. Allow to cool and then proceed as above.

Grilled turkey breast fillets with sage, lemon and pine nut pesto

We all tend to ignore turkey for most of the year until Christmas comes along. As with chicken it can be a valuable ingredient, working well with so many different flavours. It's time to ditch the cranberry sauce and head off in search of something altogether more exotic.

2 tablespoons olive oil
1 tablespoon fresh lemon juice
2 garlic cloves, peeled and crushed
   with a little salt
bunch coriander, finely chopped
bunch flat-leaf parsley, finely
   chopped
4 x 180g turkey breast fillets
salt and pepper

pesto
12 fresh sage leaves
bunch flat-leaf parsley
2 garlic cloves, peeled
1 tablespoon lightly toasted pine nuts
4 tablespoons olive oil
1 tablespoon Parmesan, grated
salt and pepper

1. Combine all the pesto ingredients except the Parmesan in a blender, season with salt and pepper and blitz. Stir in the Parmesan and check seasoning.

2. Combine the olive oil, lemon juice, garlic and herbs and toss well. Season with salt and pepper and set aside. For best results leave in the fridge overnight.

3. Preheat the grill and cook the turkey for four to five minutes on each side, or until cooked through.

4. Serve with the salsa. In Giraffe we tend to serve this with mash, rice or green beans and a wedge of lemon.

Tall tales
To toast pine nuts place in a hot frying pan over a moderate heat and toss occasionally.

Jambalaya meatballs with pasta or rice

Jambalaya in the sense of Louisiana creole. The dish comes in several guises, with or without tomatoes, cooked separately and together, with meat and without. What links them all however, is the idea of a simple, filling dish - something that is done with ease but lots of satisfaction. Meatballs are easy, and once the work is done, things simmer away rather nicely on their own. Time for a cold drink perhaps.

meatballs
400g minced lamb
400g minced chicken
1 red onion, finely diced
4 garlic cloves, peeled and finely
    chopped
bunch fresh coriander leaves,
    chopped
bunch fresh parsley, chopped
1 tablespoon Cajun spice
2 medium size potatoes, peeled
    and grated
$^1/_2$ teaspoon salt

pasta or rice
400g fettuccini or brown rice
1 red pepper, deseeded and sliced
1 green pepper, deseeded and sliced
1 yellow pepper, deseeded and sliced
1 medium sized red onion, sliced
4 tablespoons olive oil
2 teaspoons Cajun spice
2 handfuls rocket leaves
100g grated Parmesan cheese
400g marinara sauce (see page 97)

1. To make the meatballs, mix the chicken, lamb, red onion and chopped herbs. Add the grated potatoes and season the mix with salt and Cajun spice.

2. Take two tablespoon of the meatball mix and roll into a meatball. Apply oil to your hand to avoid meat sticking to your palm.

3. Add oil to hot pan and seal the meatballs. Finish the cooking in an oven at 180C/gas mark 4 for around 15 minutes.

4. Boil enough salted water to cook the pasta (or rice).

5. Add the olive oil to a hot saucepan and sauté the meatballs, onion and sliced peppers. Add the cooked pasta (or rice) and Cajun spice, toss it for a minute. Add the marinara sauce and season well. Garnish with rockets leaves and sprinkle the grated parmesan on top.

BBQ Duck fajita burrito

Duck makes a fantastic filling for burritos; rich, succulent and earthy – just what you need when you are looking for something warming and comforting.

1 tablespoon olive oil
2 duck breast
3 onions
2 each red, green and yellow peppers
4 garlic cloves, peeled and chopped
150g shitake mushrooms
salt and pepper
1 tablespoon coriander, chopped

fajita spice
1 teaspoon ground cumin
1 teaspoon ground coriander
$1/2$ teaspoon sweet paprika
2 tablespoons breadcrumbs
$1/2$ teaspoon dried oregano

mexican green rice
1 mug brown rice
2 tablespoons olive oil
2 garlic cloves, peeled and chopped
2 tablespoons fresh parsley, chopped
2 green chillies, chopped
2 tablespoons coriander, chopped

4 large tortillas
8 tablespoons adobe sauce
  (see page 13)
1 cup Monterey Jack cheese
4 tablespoons soured cream
fresh salad leaves
herby house dressing (see page 64)

1. Heat the olive oil in a pan. Season the duck breasts and fry, skin side down first, for five minutes. Turn over and carry on cooking on the other side for seven minutes or until the duck is cooked. Remove and allow to cool.

2. Slice the onions and peppers. In the remaining oil and duck fat, stir-fry the garlic, onions, peppers and mushrooms together for two to three minutes over a high flame. Season with salt and pepper. Slice the cooled duck breast and add, along with the fajita spice, and cook for a two to three minutes. Remove the pan from heat, check seasoning and stir in the coriander.

3. Cook the rice in plenty of salted boiling water for 20 minutes or until tender. When the rice is cooked, drain the excess water. Heat the oil in a saucepan. Add the chopped garlic and sauté for one minute. Add the cooked brown rice, chopped parsley, green chillies and coriander. Mix well and season with salt and pepper.

4. Place one cup of the duck mixture in the centre of each tortilla and fold both sides without overlapping. Take one open end of the tortilla and fold over. Then roll the burrito to other open end to make a parcel or square shape.

5. Place the Mexican green rice in the centre of four plates, top with the duck fajita burrito. Pour the adobe sauce on the burrito. Sprinkle some Monterey Jack cheese. Melt the cheese in the oven. Put the dollop of soured cream on top. Serve with crispy summer salad lettuce with some tequila and lime dressing.

Portuguese grilled butterflied chicken

Peri peri, piri piri or even peli peli: the spelling varies as much as the sauce, which is essentially hot and identified with Portuguese food. You will also find peri peri dishes throughout most of east Africa. The name refers to the chilli, and also to the dish, which as you can see from this recipe does not always require peri peri chillies (they can be a trifle hard to find).

peri peri sauce

1 onion, peeled and very finely chopped

5 garlic cloves, peeled and crushed with a little salt

zest of 2 lemons, juice of 3, plus 1 to serve

2 teaspoons chilli flakes

1 fresh red chilli, deseeded and finely chopped, or to taste

3 teaspoons dried oregano

2 teaspoons paprika

3 tablespoons olive oil, plus a little extra for serving

4 x 500g poussin (spring chicken), spatchcocked

2 tablespoons flat leaf parsley, chopped

1. Combine the onion, garlic, lemon zest and half the juice, chilli flakes, fresh chilli, oregano, paprika and olive oil to make a paste. Toss the poussin in a bowl with the marinade, cover and set aside in the fridge overnight.

2. Preheat the grill and cook for 12-15 minutes each side, or until cooked through. Sprinkle with the remaining lemon juice, a drizzle of olive oil and the parsley and serve with lemon wedges.

Tall tales

You could partner this with a green or tomato salad in the summer and steamed greens in the winter. Boiled or roast potatoes and rice are all suitable as the cooked meat and marinade are full of delicious juices.

Hawaiian chilli bowl

Maybe it is the sea air, the mix of cultures, the bright lively zing of lime juice, fresh vegetables and the earthy chilli but this is a dish that speaks sunshine through and through.

olive oil
1 large onion, peeled and finely
   chopped
2 garlic cloves, peeled and finely
   chopped
1kg ground beef

1 tablespoon sun-dried tomato paste
$^1/_2$ teaspoon ancho chilli powder
   (a smoky chilli powder)
1 teaspoon ground cumin
2 cinnamon sticks
1 teaspoon sweet paprika
1 teaspoon dried oregano
salt and pepper
400g tin red kidney beans, drained
   and rinsed
1 400g tin chopped tomatoes

salsa
juice of 2 limes
1 avocado, stoned and diced
1 red onion, peeled and chopped
3 tomatoes, skinned, deseeded and
   chopped
1 tablespoon coriander, chopped
20g macadamia nuts, crushed
20g small pineapple cubes

1. Place a large saucepan over a moderate heat, add four tablespoons of olive oil and then the chopped onion. Cook for 10 minutes and then add the garlic. Cook for one minute and then add the beef. Cook for a further five minutes and add the sun-dried tomato paste, ancho chilli powder, cumin, cinnamon, paprika and oregano. Season with salt and pepper, add the kidney beans and tinned tomatoes and stir so everything is well mixed. Simmer, uncovered, for an hour. You may need to add a little water, it should be moist without being soupy.

2. For the salsa combine the zest and juice from the limes with the avocado, red onion, fresh tomatoes, coriander and crushed macadamias and pineapple cubes. Spoon on top of the chilli and serve.

Tall tales

Why not embellish with a dollop of soured cream and maybe some tortillas to do some initial scooping.

Grilled or pan roasted chicken thighs with jalapeño corn lime relish

Cheap and cheerful is a phrase we are rather fond of. To some it can mean tacky but to us it's kinda cool. Something inexpensive fashioned into something that gives you a smile. It's hard to sum up our approach to food in a better way. Of course cheap doesn't mean we compromise on quality in any way. If we did, it wouldn't be cheerful.

8 bone-in chicken thighs
4 tablespoons olive oil
2 garlic cloves, peeled and finely
  chopped
2 tablespoons white wine
$^1/_2$ teaspoon thyme leaves
1 teaspoon oregano leaves
juice of 1 lemon
salt and pepper

corn lime relish
2 heads fresh corn
4 tablespoons olive oil
juice of 1 lime
juice of $^1/_2$ lemon
bunch parsley, finely chopped
jalapeño chilli, trimmed and finely
  chopped
salt and pepper

1. Combine the chicken thighs with the next six ingredients and season with salt and pepper. Toss gently but evenly so that everything is combined well. Cover and refrigerate overnight if possible.

2. Preheat the grill. For the relish, leave the corn with leaves intact and grill for 10 minutes each side or until just charred. Leave until cool enough to handle and then with an ordinary knife strip off the corn into a bowl. Add the remaining ingredients and season with salt and pepper.

3. Grill the chicken thighs for 20 minutes, turning every five minutes or until cooked. Serve with the relish. If you want to use this as a main course try with new potatoes or our onion mash on page 116.

Tall tales

Herbs can make a huge difference to everyone's cooking. They bring a freshness and vitality, a ray of sunshine. There are rules of thumb; rosemary and lamb, sage and pork, coriander and anything Eastern. But herbs are far more versatile than this suggests. Both sage and rosemary go well with chicken, and potatoes. So push your neck out and have a go. You might be pleasantly surprised.

Goat's cheese, caramelised onion and mushroom pizza tostada with rocket and pine nuts

What's a pizza? A bread base and toppings. After that it depends who is doing the talking and who is behind the pizza paddle. You can argue over pizza forever. We tend to get on with eating it and to that end, it's about a base and great toppings. Flat bread might seem like a cop-out to the purists, but hey, while they are still rolling their dough we are likely to be clearing up. Convenience can be a wonderful thing.

marinara sauce
2 cloves of garlic, crushed
4 tablespoons olive oil
1 medium white onion, diced
400g tin chopped tomatoes,
　　drained rinsed
$^1/_2$ teaspoon oregano
8-10 fresh basil leaves
salt and pepper

4 Lebanese flat bread
8 tablespoons marinara sauce
4 tablespoons goat's cheese
4 tablespoons grated mozzarella
16 cherry tomatoes
200g baby spinach leaves
1 jar artichokes, drained
8 tablespoons Parmesan shavings
salt and pepper
4 handfuls rocket leaves
4 tablespoons pesto dressing

1. Preheat the oven to 200C/gas mark 6.

2. To make the sauce – heat the olive oil in saucepan and add the crushed garlic. Add the diced onions and sauté it for 4-5 minutes until it gets soft and succulent. Mash the tomatoes with a fork or potato masher and add the chopped tomatoes, oregano and fresh basil leaves to sauce pan. Cook the sauce for 8-10 minutes.

3. Spread 8 tablespoons of the marinara sauce on the flat bread. Spread the spinach leaves on top of the sauce.

4. Cut the artichokes in half and scatter over the bread, sprinkle the crumbled goat's cheese and grated mozzarella cheese over the pizza and season with salt and pepper. Place the bread on a roasting tray and bake in the oven for 10 minutes or until the cheese is brown and bubbling.

5. Remove the pizza from the oven. Toss the rocket leaves with the pesto dressing and place it on the pizzas. Sprinkle the shaved Parmesan over the pizza and serve hot.

Spaghetti bolognese our way

While authenticity is something we respect it is not something giraffes tend to indulge in very often. It's part of our wild nature. We are not very good at following rules. Or rather, we like to challenge pretty much everything. That way we get to ensure we understand why we do things the way we do. Adding chicken to a traditional bolognese was done as a way to lighten things up, but it also adds another dimension, some complexity which we think is rather a good thing.

3 tablespoons olive oil
75g streaky bacon, finely chopped
1 onion, peeled and chopped
2 carrots, diced
2 celery sticks, chopped
450g beef mince
350g minced chicken
salt and pepper
500ml red wine
1 tablespoon balsamic vinegar
2 400g tins tomatoes
1 tablespoon Worcestershire sauce
1 teaspoon sun-dried tomato paste
2 sprigs thyme
1 teaspoon dried oregano or fresh if
   you have
400g spaghetti
Parmesan cheese, grated

1. Heat the olive oil in a large pan over a moderate heat. When hot add the bacon, onion, carrot and celery. Cook over a low heat for 20 minutes to soften but do not allow to colour.

2. Add the beef and chicken, season with salt and pepper and sauté for five minutes, stirring so the meat loses its raw colour. Add the wine and vinegar along with the tomatoes, Worcestershire sauce, sun-dried tomato paste and the herbs. Cook for 30 minutes. Check seasoning and add a little more wine or water if it gets a little dry.

3. Cook the spaghetti according to the instructions on the packet. Toss with the sauce and serve with grated Parmesan on top.

Tall tales

You can use fresh oregano but it lacks the intensity. Drying herbs doesn't really work in our experience, except with oregano, which somehow is transformed by drying.

You can use other shapes of pasta. Penne works well. It just doesn't have the same slurpability factor which we think is rather a shame.

What to have with it? Tradition dictates garlic bread, at least our tradition does. Most Italians would be horrified.

'Fire-roasted' balsamic veggie burrito

Burrito means little donkey, supposedly because of their shape. We like to think of both donkey and burrito as being rather useful to have around. The donkey to fetch and carry, the burrito as an anytime snack, the sort of thing you want a sandwich to be but it so seldom is. Packed with goodness that is satisfying and easy.

1 red onion, peeled and chopped
1 courgette, trimmed and diced
1 small aubergine, trimmed and diced
1 red chilli, finely chopped
pinch dried oregano
3 tablespoons olive oil
¹/₂ green pepper, diced
¹/₂ red pepper, diced
¹/₂ yellow pepper, diced
¹/₂ small tin sweetcorn
1 little gem lettuce, shredded
1 400g tin red kidney beans, well
   rinsed and drained
4 tablespoons adobe sauce
   (see page 13)
2 tablespoons feta cheese, crumbled
flour tortillas

1. Cook the onion, courgette, aubergine, chilli and oregano in the oil over a moderate heat for 10 minutes or until soft but not coloured.

2. Add the peppers, cook for five minutes, then add the little gem, kidney beans and adobe sauce. Cook for a further 10 minutes stirring all the time. Remove from the heat, allow to cool and stir in the feta.

3. Spoon into the tortillas, roll up, folding in the ends and serve.

Teriyaki beef rib steak with asparagus and green onions

Teriyaki means both how the sauce and the meat is marinated as well as the cooking technique; the grill. Or chargrill. Hit Toyko as offices empty and there are plenty of bars serving up teriyaki and cold beers to tired office workers. Traditionally, in Japan teriyaki cooking implies brushing the food as it cooks, which gives it a rich lacquered appearance. You can do the same here with the steak.

4 sirloin steaks
2 tablespoons teriyaki sauce
3cm piece of ginger, grated
2 garlic cloves, peeled, finely chopped
    and mashed with a little salt
20 asparagus spears
12 spring onions, trimmed but whole
    and green parts left attached

1. Combine the teriyaki sauce with the ginger and garlic. Toss the steaks so they are well coated and refrigerate overnight, or at least for a few hours.

2. Drain the steaks, lightly oil and sear on a ridged griddle pan or frying pan for three minutes or until cooked to your liking. Remove and keep warm.

3. Blanch the asparagus and spring onions in boiling salted water for three minutes, drain and refresh. Toss the spring onions and asparagus lightly in oil and sear for three to four minutes or until cooked, on a ridged griddle pan.

4. Slice the steaks thinly on the diagonal. Serve with the vegetables, a small bowl of soy sauce for dipping, wasabi and steamed jasmine or brown rice.

Tall tales

Why stop at steak? Lamb chops are rather good like this, as are chicken wings and drumsticks, although both will need slightly longer cooking. Fish, too, is good as are vegetables like aubergine, mushrooms and red onions. Skip the salt, there tends to be enough seasoning from the soy.

Roasted lamb chops with Indian curry spices, sweet potato mash and green beans

Simply grilled lamb chops are delicious, but the urge to spice them up a bit was too much for one of our chefs whose recent travels in India led to the following version. You might be tempted to call it an Indian spiced dinner as the traditional meat + potato + veg are so clearly evident. Whatever your view, we find a finger bowl is rather inevitable.

1 teaspoon fennel seeds
1 teaspoon coriander seeds
$1/2$ teaspoon black peppercorns
2 red chillies, deseeded and finely
   chopped
bunch fresh coriander, roughly
   chopped with a few leaves kept
   aside to garnish
bunch mint, chopped
2 teaspoons garam masala
$1/2$ teaspoon turmeric
6 tablespoons yoghurt
juice of 1 lemon
salt and pepper
4 Barnsley-style lamb chops or rack
   of lamb cutlets, although the latter
   will be more costly
4 medium-sized sweet potatoes
olive oil
4 handfuls green beans
2 tomatoes, deseeded and sliced

1. Lightly toast the spices in a dry frying pan over a moderate heat. Place in a pestle and mortar along with the chilli and black pepper and grind to a powder. Add the chopped herbs, garam masala, turmeric and all but two tablespoons of the yoghurt. Mix well. Add lemon juice and salt and pepper to taste.

2. Add the lamb to the mixture and gently turn so it is well coated. Set aside overnight in the fridge or for at least a few hours.

3. Preheat the oven to 180C/gas mark 4. Prick the sweet potato with a sharp knife and bake for 30 minutes or until tender, allow to cool slightly and remove the flesh. Mash with a little olive oil and season with salt and pepper. Keep warm.

4. Heat four tablespoons of olive oil in a pan over a moderate heat and fry the chops for three to four minutes each side or until cooked to your liking.

5. Cook the beans in plenty of boiling salted water for five minutes or until tender.

6. Serve the chops on top of the beans and mash and garnish with the sliced tomato, a little of the extra yoghurt and the sprigs of coriander.

Grilled chicken tacos with fresh orange salsa

Why are Giraffe's yellow? You could say it was a corporate thing. But then that is not very Giraffe. It's rather more a wish to be cheerful, a reflection of summer sunshine. An enthusiasm about being happy. This is summer sunshine on a plate. Think surfer's lunch, or Californian surfer's lunch to be precise.

2 tablespoons fresh orange juice
1 tablespoon honey
4 chicken breasts
salt and pepper
2 chipotle chillies or to taste, chopped

orange salsa
1 orange, separated into segments
$^1/_2$ red pepper, deseeded and cut into thin slices
$^1/_2$ yellow pepper, deseeded and cut into thin slices
1 red chilli, trimmed and finely chopped
bunch coriander, roughly chopped
1 teaspoon cider vinegar
1 tablespoon honey
salt and pepper
1 iceburg lettuce, shredded

corn tortillas or taco shells
guacamole

1. Combine the orange juice and honey. Season the chicken with salt and pepper and toss in the honey mixture along with the chillies. Set aside, or overnight in the fridge if possible.

2. Preheat the grill. Remove the chicken from the marinade and grill for six to seven minutes on each side or until cooked. Allow to rest under some tin foil for five minutes and then slice on the diagonal.

3. Combine the orange segments with the peppers, chilli, coriander, vinegar and honey and season with salt and pepper.

4. Warm the taco shells or tortillas by wrapping in tin foil and leaving under the grill.

5. Spoon guacamole into the tacos or tortillas, add the lettuce, top with the chicken and then the salsa and serve.

Jungle Curry

Banish any thoughts of something searingly hot. This is a curry with lots of vegetables, a great deal of colour and vibrancy. Just like the jungle really. How much chilli you use is up to you.

1 small onion, peeled and grated
3 garlic cloves, peeled and grated
3cm fresh galangal, peeled and grated
3cm fresh ginger, peeled and grated
1 stick fresh lemon-grass, tough outside leaves removed and soft interior finely chopped
1 red chilli, trimmed and finely chopped (or to taste)
6 tablespoons vegetable oil
1 bunch coriander, roots and stems finely chopped and leaves reserved
5 fresh kaffir lime leaves
1 tablespoon ground cumin
1 tablespoon ground coriander
half teaspoon turmeric
1 tablespoons tomato puree
1 litre vegetable stock
2 tablespoons soy sauce
1 small aubergine, cut into bite-sized pieces
1 small butternut squash cut into 3cm chunks
2 tablespoons tofu, cut into bite-sized pieces
1 handful sugar snaps
1 handful tinned bamboo shoots, well rinsed and drained

1. Fry the onion, garlic, galangal, ginger, lemongrass and chilli in two tablespoons of the vegetable oil over a moderate heat for two minutes or until just coloured. Add the coriander root, lime leaves and spices and cook for two minutes or until the spices loose their raw aroma. Add the tomato puree. Cook for a further five minutes. Add the vegetable stock and cook for 10 minutes. Add the soy sauce. Check seasoning, you may need a little salt.

2. Toss the aubergine in two of the remaining tablespoons of vegetables oil. Season and grill until golden brown and soft.

3. Heat the remaining vegetable oil and lightly fry the tofu until just coloured.

4. Add the aubergine and tofu along with the butternut squash, sugar snaps and bamboo shoots to the curry, bring to the boil, lower the heat and simmer for 10 to 15 minutes or until the butternut squash is tender.

5. Check seasoning, stir in the reserved coriander leaves and serve with plain rice.

Easy open-faced chicken cordon bleu

With cordon bleu you season and stuff, anything from chicken to veal, beef and even vegetables. But at Giraffe we think life is a little too short to stuff. We like the idea, but if you ask a giraffe what the difference is between folding and stuffing they'll tell you there isn't much in it. So kick back and fold and let your imagination run riot over tantalising combinations.

4 chicken breasts, battered out
   to 1cm thick
12 slices of Serrano or Parma ham
handful spinach leaves
100g gruyere cheese, grated
1 tablespoon butter
2 tablespoons olive oil
salt and pepper
wedge of lemon

1. Season the chicken with salt and pepper. Lay a couple of slices of ham over each chicken breast. Divide up the spinach and place in the centre of each breast. Scatter over the cheese and fold in half.

2. Heat the butter and oil in a shallow pan over a low heat. Season the chicken on the outside and slide into the pan. Cook for five minutes on each side or until cooked through and the cheese has melted.

3. Serve with the juices from the pan and a lemon wedge.

Tall tales

Cured ham comes in many forms. Parma maybe the most famous ham but there are many more to be found in Italy. Spain, too, produces excellent ham – just try the highly prized and rather delicious Jabugo ham. Which one to choose is a matter of personal preference.

This recipe also works well with beef, and particularly well with veal. You could use rocket in place of spinach to give everything a slightly more peppery flavour.

Farmers' market vegetable layered lasagne

Pasta may be the preferred route for most, but flour and water – ok without the eggs – is what a tortilla is all about. Simple, honest and good. And when you slip tortillas in place of sheets of lasagne, you have an equally good result, albeit a little different. It might make Italians scream in horror but we reckon the proof is in the eating and as we watch hundreds of these being gobbled up each year, who are we to judge.

4 tablespoons olive oil
4 leeks, sliced
salt and pepper
1kg spinach
2 garlic cloves, skinned and finely chopped
400g goat's cheese, crumbled
1 jar artichokes, drained and quartered
150g cheddar cheese, thinly sliced
8 tortillas

1. Heat the olive oil in a large pan and when hot add the leeks, turn the heat down and simmer for 10 minutes or until soft. Season with salt and pepper. Add the spinach and wilt down. This should take about five minutes. Add the garlic, toss well and check seasoning.

2. Spread a layer of spinach in a shallow oven-proof dish, scatter over some of the goat's cheese and a few artichokes and layer in the tortillas, taking care not to overlap. Repeat with the spinach, goat's cheese, artichoke and tortilla, finishing up with the tortilla and then layer on
the cheddar.

3. Bake in a preheated oven, 180C/gas mark 4 for 30 minutes or until brown and bubbling.

4. We serve this topped with a little lightly dressed rocket but we are often asked for garlic bread or chips, both of which are rather good.

Tall tales

If you find goat's cheese a little too rich try making this with ricotta. You might find a tablespoon or two of parmesan is needed to pep things up a bit. Ricotta, although delicious, can be a tad bland.

Oz burger

The idea of a lot of giraffes sitting about talking about burgers may seem an odd one but we kinda encourage that sort of thing. It leads to innovation, a sense of community, a sharing of ideas. This version of a burger has proved rather popular with customers and came from a handful of Ozzie staff via Bondi Beach. Global inspiration of the best kind. If the weather permits you, gain extra oomph using the barbecue or if you have a chargrill or ridged griddle, so much the better.

800g ground beef
salt and pepper
ketchup to taste
chilli paste to taste
4 tablespoons mayonnaise
4 thick slices pineapple, central core
    removed
sugar
vegetable oil
4 eggs
4 buns, toasted
cooked (not pickled) beetroot, sliced
4 slices lettuce
4 slices tomato
4 slices red onion

1. Preheat the grill.

2. Season the beef with salt and pepper and mould into four burgers. Set aside.

3. Combine the ketchup, chilli paste and mayo.

4. Sprinkle each of the pineapple rings with a teaspoon of sugar – make sure to do both sides. Grill until caramalised.

5. Heat a tablespoon of vegetable oil and fry (or grill or barbecue) the burgers for a good 15 minutes turning every three or four minutes so they are cooked on both sides. Remove and allow to rest. Fry the eggs.

6. Assemble the burger by spreading the mayo/ketchup combination on toasted buns. Build from the bottom up, starting with the burger so the juices run into the bread, then the pineapple, beetroot slice, fried egg, lettuce, tomato and red onion. Top and serve.

Tall tales

Cooking burgers is something of a challenge. How to cook the inside without burning the outside is something anyone choosing to barbecue burgers during the summer will know only too well. Restaurants will often colour a burger either on a griddle plate or in a frying pan and then transfer it to the oven to finish cooking. If you have an oven proof pan this is very easy to replicate at home. And means you can put your feet up while your burgers are cooking.

Moorish grilled beef burger

While Giraffe is far from being a burger bar we like our burgers. There is something unfussy and easy that we like about them. You can use a knife and fork if you like but we kinda like the hands-on approach, it brings a more complete burger experience. The Moors brought a lot of interesting ingredients into Spain, an early go at global food which was a bit of a hit.

800g minced beef or turkey
salt and pepper
4 buns
4 slices Manchego cheese
4 slices Serrano ham
2 tomatoes, sliced
1 jar piquillo peppers

4 tablespoons mayonnaise
2 cloves of garlic, peeled and crushed
  with a little salt
2 teaspoons hot paprika

1. Preheat the grill or griddle pan and preheat the oven to 180C/gas mark 4.

2. Season the meat with salt and pepper, mix with your hands and then shape into four burgers.

3. Grill for two to three minutes on each side until lightly coloured, transfer to finish cooking in the oven for eight to 10 minutes or until done.

4. Whisk the garlic and paprika into the mayonnaise.

5. Build the burgers at the table or in advance as you like. We are a bit particular about it but it's a Giraffe thing; bun, a little mayo, burger, cheese, ham, tomato, peppers and a little more mayo before the bun. No surprises perhaps, but the eating is pretty good, or so we like to think.

Tall tales

Paprika comes in two shapes, hot and sweet. You sometimes hear people talking about smoked paprika but that is something of a tautology as all paprika is smoked. The peppers can be sweet or hot which decides on the final style. This is a spice that is well worth sourcing from an ethnic store. Generic paprika is dusty and dull, something the Moors would not have been pleased about.

Falafel burger

Falafals are a staple in the Middle East. With good reason. Packed full of vegetarian goodness they work as snack, meal or in a sandwich. Which is kind of how we got to the burger. You might have falafals in flat bread while gazing out over the Mediterranean but we thought the burger suited where we are at; simple good tasty food that is easy.

falafel
300g chickpeas
1 teaspoon bicarbonate of soda
5 garlic cloves, peeled
1 onion, peeled and chopped
1 leek, trimmed and chopped
generous handful coriander, chopped
1 teaspoon ground cumin
1 teaspoon ground allspice
pinch cayenne pepper
salt and pepper
vegetable oil

200g tinned roasted red peppers
160g halloumi
120g hummus
4 soft buns
120g tzatiziki
60g beetroot, grated
60g rocket
40g harissa

1. Soak the chickpeas overnight with the bicarbonate of soda. Rinse well under plenty of running water and drain. Place in a liquidiser with the next seven ingredients and blitz to a paste. Scoop into a bowl, check seasoning and leave to rest for 30 minutes.

2. Now you can either shape into traditional falafel shapes, about 4 centimetres in diameter with tapered edges or make into burgers.

3. Heat enough oil in a pan to give a depth of three centimetres. To see if it is hot enough dip a falafel in, if it sizzles the oil is ready. Cook until golden, turn over, repeat on the other side and drain on kitchen paper.

4. Grill the peppers and the cheese. Spread hummus on both the top and bottom of the bun. To build the burger put the falafel balls on the bottom, then tzatziki, red pepper, halloumi, beetroot and top with rocket. Serve with fries and harrissa on the side.

6

Fresh Fish Flavours

Fish and chips, fish and salad, fish and vegetables. Variety comes thick and fast. We stick to sustainable fish in the restaurants. We think it's a good idea to leave overfished stocks well alone so we focus on the likes of salmon, barramundi, sea bream and sea bass. We like tuna too, but not the endangered varieties.

You can put fish in a curry and we certainly do, but on the whole we tend to serve fish simply cooked and with a salsa or relish; something fresh and colourful, herb or spice laden and easy to prepare. You can get all old-fashioned with your saucing for fish but we really don't see the point.

Keep things easy and simple. A barbecue in the summer, a grill in the winter. That way cooking is kept to a minimum and the flavour of the fish shines through.

ALL RECIPES SERVE 4.

Jerk fish with lime and garlic jerk butter

Jerk seasoning is traditionally associated with pork and goat, the latter a popular meat in Jamaica, which is the home of jerk cooking. Dark forbidding meat cooked over charcoal is not really very Giraffe, so we ended up working with fish and playing with the spicing.

jerk seasoning
3 spring onions
$^1/_2$ red pepper, trimmed and chopped
1 teaspoon ground allspice
$^1/_2$ teaspoon picked thyme leaves
$^1/_2$ teaspoon ground cinnamon
$1/4$ nutmeg, grated
1 tablespoon brown sugar
1 tablespoon malt vinegar
salt and pepper
olive oil

jerk lime butter
80g softened butter
2 garlic cloves, peeled and crushed
1 tablespoon jerk seasoning
juice and zest of 1 lime
bunch coriander, chopped
bunch parsley, chopped
lime zest

4 x 180g fillets firm fish like snapper, monkfish, barramundi
juice of 1 lime

coconut and green onion rice
2 mugs rice
bunch spring onions cut into 2cm pieces
2 tablespoons vegetable oil
2 tablespoons freshly grated coconut

1. Combine all the ingredients for the jerk paste and season with salt and pepper. Whisk in enough oil to form a paste. Set aside.

2. Combine the ingredients for the butter and mix well. Set aside.

3. Wash the fish and dry with kitchen paper. Gently toss with the lime juice and combine with the jerk seasoning. Marinate for one hour and no more.

4. Preheat the grill. Cook the fish for three to four minutes on each side or until cooked through. Serve with a slice of jerk butter and coconut and green onion rice.

coconut and green onion rice

1. Cook the rice in plenty of well salted boiling water until cooked.

2. Sauté the spring onions in the vegtable oil until tender, about four minutes. Combine with the cooked rice and the coconut and check seasoning.

Russel's crab and chilli pasta

There are many who swoon at lobster and although it may be the king of the sea, crab is where the action really is. Sweet, saline, meaty and altogether unmistakable in flavour, it is a perfect partner with pasta. You can pick a whole crab if you have time, but packets of crab meat are now easy to find. After that, some judicious seasoning and assembly and supper is on the table.

olive oil
1 red onion, peeled and finely
    chopped
1 teaspoon red chilli flakes (or to
    taste)
1 red chilli, deseeded and finely
    chopped
2 garlic cloves, peeled, chopped and
    crushed with a little salt
12 cherry tomatoes quartered
$^1/_2$ teaspoon dried oregano
salt and pepper
$^1/_2$ glass white wine
400g spaghetti
200g fresh, picked crab meat
bunch flat-leaf parsley, chopped
juice of 1 lemon

1. Heat three tablespoons of olive oil in a frying pan over a moderate heat. Add the onion and cook for 10 minutes without colouring. Add the chilli flakes and fresh chilli, cook for two minutes. Add the garlic, tomatoes and oregano and season with salt and pepper. Cook for two minutes and then add the white wine. Cook for two minutes.

2. Stir in the crab meat, parsley, lemon juice and season with salt and pepper to taste. Cook the pasta in plenty of well-salted water, drain and add to the sauce.

Tall tales

Other things to do with crab meat:
Make into potato cakes.
Spread on garlic-rubbed toast and douse with olive oil.
Mix with mayonnaise and have with crusty bread.

Other pastas:
Linguini is popular in Italy
Also spaghettini, which is a thinner version of spaghetti

Grilled Marrakesh-spiced sea bass, herby green onion mash and cherry tomato salad

A meaty fish like sea bass responds well to spices. The skin will crisp up and adds real depth of flavour to the overall dish, but if this doesn't tempt it is easy enough to remove and set aside.

1 teaspoon cumin seeds
1 teaspoon coriander seeds
1/4 teaspoon turmeric
pinch paprika
pinch cayenne
pinch cinnamon
salt and pepper
4 flllets sea bass (about 160g each)
olive oil

herby mash
4 potatoes, peeled and cut into
    chunks
25g butter or three tablespoons
olive oil
150ml full fat milk
6 spring onions, trimmed and finely
    chopped
1 tablespoon each roughly chopped
    parsley, chervil
and tarragon

1. Grind the spices. Season the fish with salt and pepper on the flesh side and sprinkle with the spices to coat fish. Gently rub in. Set aside for 20 minutes or even overnight in the fridge if possible.

2. Lightly oil the fish and place skin-side up, under a preheated grill for six to seven minutes or until cooked.

3. For the cherry tomato salad halve the cherry tomatoes, season with salt and pepper and mix with three tablespoons of olive oil and toss gently.

herby mash

1. Cook the potatoes in plenty of salted water until tender. Drain and mash.

2. You can hold them at this point, covered with clingfilm in the fridge.

3. Put the potatoes in a saucepan over a low heat and stir in the butter (or olive oil), milk and spring onions. Heat through, check seasoning and add the chopped herbs just before serving.

Tall tales
Other fish to spice up include sea bream, tuna, halibut, mackerel and snapper.

BBQ salmon trout with yellow pepper and coriander salsa

As you can see from the method there is not much to this dish. Gather the ingredients together, combine and off you go, supper on the table. Simplicity and honesty is very Giraffe, it cuts out all the fuss and lets us focus on what is important.

BBQ sauce
2 teaspoons sweet paprika
½ teaspoon chilli powder (or to taste)
1 teaspoon ground cumin
2 tablespoons dried oregano
1 tablespoon dark brown sugar
salt and pepper
juice of 1 lemon
2 tablespoons olive oil

4 x 180g fillets of salmon trout

salsa
1 yellow pepper cut into bite-sized cubes
1 garlic clove, peeled and finely chopped
1 tablespoon toasted pine nuts
bunch coriander, chopped
bunch flat-leaf parsley, chopped
2 tablespoons olive oil
juice of half a lemon
salt and pepper

herby rice
2 cups brown rice
2 tablespoons olive oil
2 garlic cloves, peeled and chopped
2 tablespoons fresh parsley, chopped
2 green chillies, trimmed and chopped
2 tablespoons fresh coriander, chopped
salt and pepper

1. Combine the first eight ingredients for the BBQ sauce. Rub and brush over the fish. Set aside.

2. Combine all the ingredients for the salsa. Taste and adjust seasoning.

3. Grill or pan-fry the fish for two to three minutes each side – the inside should be a little pink – brushing with the BBQ rub as you go.

4. Serve with a scoop of salsa on top.

on the side herby rice

1. Cook the rice in plenty of salted boiling water for 20 minutes or until tender. When the rice is cooked, drain the excess water.

2. Heat the oil in a saucepan. Add the chopped garlic and sauté for one minute. Add the cooked brown rice, chopped parsley, green chillies and coriander. Mix well, heat through and season with salt and pepper.

Miso-lime salmon with wasabi rice and green onions

Ask a giraffe about miso and the answer is likely to be long, complicated and open-ended. Miso is a pretty generic term for a traditional Japanese seasoning produced by fermenting rice and either barley or soybeans with salt and a fungus called kojikin. The resulting paste has an earthy, fruity, savoury characteristic but much depends on which brand you go for and a lot is down to preference. Reach out and try, like any good giraffe.

salt
2 mugs brown rice
25g miso paste
zest and juice of two limes plus one for serving
1 teaspoon toasted sesame seeds
1 teaspoon mirin
grinding of black pepper
4 salmon darnes (the middle cut)
3 tablespoons vegetable oil
1 teaspoon wasabi paste (or to taste)
4 spring onions, finely sliced at 45 degrees
2 tablespoons fresh coriander, chopped
1 lime, quartered

1. Cook the rice in plenty of well-salted boiling water for 15-20 minutes or until tender. Drain, refresh under cold water and drain again.

2. Combine the miso paste with the lime juice and zest, sesame seeds, mirin and black pepper. Turn the salmon darnes in this mixture making sure the fish is well coated. Set aside, turning occasionally.

3. Heat a large frying pan or wok and when smoking add the vegetable oil, quickly followed by the rice. Stir-fry for three to four minutes or until well heated through. Remove from the heat and fold in wasabi paste, season with salt and mix well. Stir in the spring onions and coriander.

4. Grill the salmon for three minutes each side or until cooked through and serve on top of the rice with a lime wedge.

Grilled sea bream with dill chimichurri

A sauce made from lots of chopped fresh herbs. The chimichurri also goes well with grilled meat and chicken.

1 green chilli, deseeded and finely chopped
$1/2$ a teaspoon ground cumin
3 tablespoons dill, finely chopped
1 garlic clove, peeled and finely chopped
2 tablespoons parsley, finely chopped
1 tablespoon tarragon, roughly chopped
3 tablespoons white wine vinegar
juice of 1 lemon
2 sea bream, filleted
olive oil
salt and pepper

1. Combine the first seven ingredients with the juice from the lemon, season and set aside.

2. Season the fish with salt and pepper, rub with a little olive oil and barbecue, grill or fry for two to three minutes on each side or until cooked through.

3. Serve with a spoonful of the chimichurri and grilled vegetables or boiled new potatoes.

Tall tales
Sea bass also works well with this dish, or you could try gurnard, a lesser-known but plentiful fish with a good meaty texture.

Cajun pan-seared salmon with fire-roasted corn salsa

This salmon is full of punch and has a spiky, globally influenced sauce to go with it. You could of course buy Cajun sauce in a jar but that's not the Giraffe way. We're all about food with life and attitude, which means mixing your own sauce from scratch. You'll also make a different sauce every time – which, as any giraffe will tell you, is a good thing.

4 tablespoons olive oil
1 teaspoon each mixed dried herbs and spices (for example ground coriander, cumin, thyme and oregano)
2 garlic cloves, peeled and crushed with a little salt
2 teaspoons hot paprika
juice of 1 lemon
4 x 150g skinless salmon fillets
lime wedges
salt and pepper

salsa
4 tablespoons olive oil
2 fresh heads corn, stripped of their husks
1 red pepper
1 red chilli
3 spring onions
juice of 1 lime
1 avocado, diced
salt and pepper
bunch coriander
bunch parsley, chopped

1. Combine the first five ingredients. Gently toss the salmon into the spicing and set aside.

2. Heat a ridged griddle or conventional grill. Grill the corn, red pepper, chilli and spring onions until lightly charred. Allow to cool and then roughly chop, removing seeds and core where relevant. Combine with the lime juice and avocado and season with salt and pepper.

3. Grill the salmon for three to four minutes on each side or until cooked (it is better a little pink in the middle). Toss the coriander and parsley through the salsa, check seasoning and serve with a lime wedge.

Tall tales

The ease of farming salmon has led to it becoming a relatively inexpensive fish. Quality varies, however, so you need to know your supplier.

Baja style white fish tacos with citrus and cucumber salsa

Baja is a region in the north west of Mexico that butts right up against California. We think this is rather a good thing as you get a combination of the best of both worlds. A laid back holiday feel which is reflected in the food. Think Hawaiian shirts, bright cocktails and beach parties. Very Giraffe really.

salsa
2 Lebanese cucumbers, trimmed and grated
4 plum tomatoes, deseeded and chopped
1 red onion, peeled and finely chopped
1/2 small white cabbage, cored and finely shredded
juice of one orange
juice of half grapefruit
juice of one lime
salt and pepper
4 tablespoons olive oil plus a little more for the fish
bunch coriander, roughly chopped
1 red chilli, trimmed and finely sliced
bunch flat-leaf parsley finely chopped

8 corn tortillas
2 ripe avocado
juice of 1/2 a lemon
600g sea bream, filleted and skin removed

chipotle aoili
250ml mayonnaise
1 garlic cloves, peeled, chopped and mashed with a little salt
generous splash chipotle Tabasco
1/2 lemon, zested and juiced

Combine all the ingredients, season with salt and pepper.

1. Combine the first four ingredients for the salsa with the orange, grapefruit and lime juice, season with salt and pepper, add the olive oil, toss well and set aside. Preheat the grill. Wrap the tortillas in tin foil and place on a shelf below the grill to heat through.

2. To prepare avocado mixture take out flesh of one avocado, season with salt and pepper and mash lightly. Stir in a squeeze of lemon juice to stop it going brown.

3. To make the salsa, slice the remaining avocado in half and cut into small cubes. Add to the tomato mixture with the chillies, herbs and lime juice. Stir gently to combine and add salt to taste.

4. Drizzle the fish with olive oil and season with salt and pepper. Grill for two minutes each side, or until cooked.

5. Spread the avocado mixture on top of tortilla. Add the fish, spoon over the aioli and fold in half. Serve with salsa.

Grilled salmon burger with Asian-style avocado salsa

Beef burger, chicken burger, why not a fish burger? We even have a falafel burger at Giraffe (see page 110). Salmon's succulence lends itself to being burgered rather well. You can use other fish but they need to be relatively oily or the burger tends to dry out. Tuna works particularly well.

salsa
1 avocado cubed
1 tablespoon soy sauce
1 tablespoon mirin
2 teaspoons toasted sesame seeds
1 tablespoon fresh horseradish, grated
handful watercress
1 tablespoon flat-leaf parsley, finely chopped
4 spring onions, finely chopped
8 radishes, diced
1 tablespoon toasted sesame oil
2 tablespoons vegetable oil
salt and pepper

600g salmon, boned
juice of 1 lemon
4 burger buns
mayonnaise
wasabi paste
4 leaves of romaine lettuce
1 beef tomato, sliced
$1/2$ red onion, peeled and finely sliced

1. Combine all the ingredients for the salsa, season with salt and pepper and set aside.

2. Preheat the grill.

3. Chop the salmon with a large sharp knife. As you progress, the salmon will start to combine and become more minced than chopped, so be patient. Season with the lemon juice and salt and pepper and mould into burgers. It helps if you dip your hands into cold water so the fish doesn't stick.

4. Toast the burger buns and spread with wasabi and mayonnaise. Stack with lettuce, tomato and red onion.

5. Grill the salmon burgers for five to six minutes each side or until cooked through. Place in the buns with the other ingredients and serve with chips or a raw veggie salad like the Powerfood salad on page 69.

Tall tales

Other fish to spice up include sea bream, tuna, halibut, mackerel and snapper.

Other ways to serve? Why not try couscous and rocket salad, and minted yoghurt.

Grilled red snapper with Indian spices and cucumber raita and watercress salad

Spiced fish? Something meaty and robust like red snapper is just the thing for this. How long to marinate? Ideally overnight in the fridge wrapped in clingfilm. But if time is short don't worry, 20 minutes will give you a flavour of India.

4 teaspoons garam masala
4 fillets red snapper, each weighing around 180g

raita
4 tablespoons yoghurt
1 tablespoon coriander, roughly chopped
1 tablespoon cucumber, diced
1 tomato, deseeded and thinly sliced

1 tablespoon olive oil
4 handfuls watercress
herby rice (see page 117)
1 lemon, quartered

1. Preheat the grill.

2. Spread the garam masala on the flesh side of the fish and set aside.

3. To make the raita, combine the yoghurt with the coriander, cucumber and tomato and season with a little salt.

4. Brush the fish with a little oil, season with salt and pepper and grill for two minutes on the flesh side, then turn and grill for two to three minutes on the skin side or until crisp and cooked through.

5. Serve on top of the herby rice, with a dollop of raita, a handful of watercress and a wedge of lemon

Tall tales

Garam masala is a mix of spices and each household in India would often have their own preferred combination. You can buy garam masala, but if you make your own not only will it be fresher, you can vary the spices used to suit your preference.

Smoked haddock and salmon fishcakes with chipotle veggie slaw

You can fishcake with pretty much any fish. Cod is a favourite (think of fishfingers), plaice and lemon sole also lend themselves to the treatment with style and panache. But the point of a fishcake is really to bring together a combination. In one corner we have the delightfully delicate haddock, given added oomph courtesy of a few rounds in the smokehouse. In the other corner we have the king of the sea, the mighty and meaty salmon. Bring them together with some fluffy potato, a bit of TLC and a generous seasoning and you get one of those dreamy marriages.

250g salmon
200 smoked haddock
300g potatoes, peeled and cubed
4 spring onions finely sliced
4 tablespoons flat-leaf parsley
2 tablespoons chopped coriander
1/2 tablespoons wholegrain mustard
1 teaspoon paprika
small tin sweetcorn
zest and juice of 1 lemon
salt and pepper

veggie slaw
250g mayonnaise
1 tablespoon tomato ketchup
1 teaspoon Worcestershire sauce
2 chipotle chillies, finely sliced
juice and zest of 1 lemon
1 tablespoon coriander, chopped
1/2 a napa cabbage, shredded
1/4 of a small red cabbage, shredded
bunch radishes, finely sliced
1 small red onion, peeled and finely
  sliced

1. In a shallow pan lightly poach the fish in salted boiling water over a low heat. Remove, allow to cool and flake. Cover the potatoes with cold water, season with salt, bring to the boil and simmer until tender. Set aside to cool and mash.

2. Combine the fish, potatoes, spring onions, parsley, coriander, mustard, paprika, sweetcorn and lemon juice and zest, and season with salt and pepper. Form into cakes.

3. For the slaw, combine all the ingredients, season with salt and pepper and toss so everything is well coated.

4. Preheat the oven to 200C/gas mark 6. Lightly oil a frying pan, sauté the cakes until just coloured and transfer to the oven for 20 minutes to heat through. Serve with the slaw.

7
Happy endings

Smiling is very important
to Giraffe. We like happiness, it's kinda
one of those essential ingredients that keeps
us all going. And if you are in the mood for something
sweet, it's important for it to be a visual treat as much as
satisfying your sweet tooth.

We are a bit retro when it comes to the dishes we like – sundaes,
pancakes, crumbles and our biggest selling dessert, the banana waffle.
We think it's a comfort thing, at least it is for us. Somehow these are
the things customers seem to want to eat; fruity, creamy assemblies of
deliciousness. Most are open to variation, so we've suggested alternatives.

We are often asked for one dessert and several spoons, casual sharing
is to be encouraged. And while we have shown several dishes
in individual portions you can always opt for a bowl in
the middle of the table. That way it's easier to
reach for a little more. Which often results in a
welcome smile.

ALL RECIPES SERVE 4.

Chocolate and strawberry pancakes, rum chocolate sauce and crème fraiche

Soft pancakes, juicy stawberries and oozing, rich, chocolate sauce. Simple indulgence perhaps, but once everything is stacked up this looks like a pile of summer sunshine and tastes like it too. If you are feeding children leaving out the rum is not going to alter things significantly.

175g self-raising flour
25g cocoa powder
50g sugar
1 teaspoon bicarbonate of soda
50g melted butter
2 eggs
500ml full fat milk
vegetable oil
200g strawberries, hulled and halved
icing sugar
200g crème fraiche

chocolate sauce
200g dark chocolate
25g sugar
50ml dark rum
25g butter

1. Mix flour, cocoa, sugar and bicarbonate of soda in one bowl. Combine the butter, eggs and half the milk in a second bowl. Pour the wet ingredients into the dry ingredients and mix well so everything is combined.

2. Heat a non-stick frying pan and drop in a spoonful of mixture. As it spreads out it will set and you can add another one. Leave space for them to spread out so they don't touch. Cook for one minute and then flip over. Keep warm in a low oven till you have cooked them all.

3. Bring the remaining 250ml of milk to the boil. Add the chocolate, sugar and rum and whisk until the chocolate has melted. Remove from the heat and whisk in the butter.

4. Stack the pancakes with strawberries, pour over the chocolate sauce and scatter over some more strawberries. Dust with icing sugar and serve with the crème fraiche.

Tall tales

If your strawberries are a little on the tart/hard side try combining with a teaspoon of sugar and a couple of teaspoons of lemon juice. Toss and leave aside for an hour or so.

Peach and blackberry sundae

There is something very celebratory about a sundae. Maybe its all that colour, the height, the layers. Or maybe its more to do with how outrageously brash it looks. Or the idea that somehow its sheer indulgence. Whatever the secret, this version brings a smile to most customers who order it.

150g crumble topping
 (see page 137)
4 peaches, halved and stoned
200g sugar
zest and juice of 1 orange
1 tablespoon Cointreau (optional)
350g blackberries (frozen are ok to
 use here)
8 scoops vanilla ice-cream
4 strawberries
4 sprigs mint
icing sugar

1. Preheat the oven to 180/gas mark 4.

2. Spread the crumble mixture out on a baking tray and bake for 20 minutes or until golden brown.

3. Combine the peaches with 350ml of water and 100g of the sugar and the orange and Cointreau in a saucepan over a low heat for 10 minutes or until the peaches just start to collapse

4. Combine the blackberries with the remaining sugar in a saucepan over a moderate heat. As soon as the blackberries start to collapse remove and set aside. Boil the liquid until it just starts to become syrupy. Remove from the heat and return the blackberries.

5. Place a tablespoon of the blackberry compote in the bottom of four sundae glasses, then a scoop of ice-cream, then half a peach and sprinkle with some of the crumble topping. Repeat. Top with a strawberry and sprig of mint and dust with icing sugar.

Tall tales

Raspberries also work. Indeed most berries. As you are cooking them down frozen are ok. Don't skimp on the peaches though, they need to be big and juicy and full of summer sunshine.

Sticky toffee pudding

Indulgent, rich, a classic. What can we say? This is just one of those puddings which, if you are in the mood, hits the spot. We sell hundreds of them every week, even in the height of summer.

1 teaspoon bicarbonate of soda
360g butter, softened
480g dark brown sugar
3 eggs
750g plain flour
1 ¹/₂ teaspoons baking powder
150g sultanas

toffee sauce
200g dark brown sugar
200ml double cream

1. Preheat the oven to 180C/gas mark 4.

2. Bring 500ml water to the boil, add the bicarbonate of soda and set aside.

3. Whisk the butter and sugar and beat in the eggs. Fold in the flour, baking powder and sultanas. Stir in the reserved water.

4. Line a baking tray with greaseproof paper, spoon in the mixture and cover with tin foil. Bake for 50 minutes or until the mixture is cooked (an inserted skewer should come out clean).

5. Leave to cool for five minutes and turn out on to a chopping board. Remove the greaseproof and cut into squares.

6. Combine the sugar with 200ml of water and cook over a moderate heat until caramel point is reached (the mixture is a dark mahogany brown). Remove from the heat and allow to cool for a couple of minutes. Add the cream and mix together. Take care as the mixture tends to bubble up. You may need to return to the heat briefly and add some water.

7. Serve the pudding with the toffee sauce over the top and dare we say it, a lot more cream or ice-cream.

Easy chocolate chip, Baileys and banana fool with wafers

This is an easy and quick pud for adults and without the Bailey's is pretty good for smaller guests too.

100g dark chocolate
10g cocoa powder, sifted
40g icing sugar, sifted
500ml double cream, whipped
25ml Baileys
20g dark chocolate chips
2 ripe bananas, peeled and chopped

filo wafers
5 sheets filo pastry
100g unsalted butter, melted
icing sugar

1. Place the chocolate in a bowl over a saucepan of boiling water. Stir and melt. Remove from the heat and stir in the cocoa powder and icing sugar. Fold into the whipped cream. Add the Baileys, chocolate chips and bananas and stir gently so everything is well combined but take care not to knock the air out of the cream.

2. Preheat the oven to 180C/gas mark 4. Lay a sheet of filo pastry out on your work surface, brush with a little melted butter and dust with icing sugar. Repeat with the other sheets. Cut into triangles and bake for 10 minutes or until golden brown. Allow to cool.

Tall tales

Dark rum also works well in place of the Bailey's.

If the filo wafers are a step too far a packet of shortbread biscuits has been known to go down rather well. Its a crunch thing so don't feel guilty.

In the summer you can add in strawberries, chopped peaches or raspberries for a lighter feel.

Apple and passionfruit crumble

We are as partial to a traditional crumble as the next person. Old-fashioned comfort at its best. Mix in a little passionfruit however, and you will be amazed at the difference it makes. Zing springs to mind, a kind of playfulness we are rather keen on.

5 large cooking apples, peeled
  and cored
50g butter
250g caster sugar
zest of 1 orange
zest of 1 lemon
6 passionfruit, halved and pulp
  scooped out
100g chilled butter, diced
175g flour
25g ground almonds
100g soft brown sugar
60g flaked almonds, chopped
60g porridge oats

1. Peel, core and cut the apple in dice. Melt the butter in a saucepan and add the apples, sugar, orange and lemon zest and 60ml of water. Cook gently for 10-15 minutes or until soft. Remove from the heat and stir in the passionfruit. Spoon into an ovenproof bowl.

2. Combine the remaining ingredients and rub everything in together using your finger tips. Scatter over the fruit filling and transfer to a preheated oven, 180C/gas mark 4 until golden brown, about 40 minutes. Can be served with cream or ice-cream.

Tall tales

A crumble topping is easily varied using different nuts. Hazel, walnut, brazil are all good. Peanuts are not so good. We tried them once but the smile we like to see didn't materialise. If you are feeling flush pine nuts do work deliciously well.

Orange and ginger French toast with caramelised pineapple

French toast is one of those oh-so-simple inventions it's hard to imagine life with out it. While an easy win for breakfast in its plain form, it can be dressed up for a sweet finish with ease. Citrus fruits work particularly well and this caramelised pineapple is a favourite, particularly when other fruits are difficult to find.

55g butter
350g pineapple, cut into 2cm chunks
2 tablespoons light soft brown sugar
juice of 1 lime
4 thick slices brioche bread
2 eggs, beaten
4 tablespoons single cream
zest and juice of 1 orange
1 tablespoon caster sugar
1 teaspoon fresh ginger, grated
200ml crème fraiche

1. Heat a frying pan and add 25g of the butter. When it starts to froth add the pineapple, toss lightly to heat through and sprinkle in the sugar. Cook over a moderate heat until it starts to caramelise. It will darken in colour and when it is mahogany brown remove from the heat and squeeze over the lime juice.

2. Whisk the eggs, cream, orange, sugar and ginger in a shallow bowl. Heat a shallow frying pan and when hot add the remaining butter. Dip the brioche into the egg mixture briefly. As the butter froths slide the brioche slices in and cook for two minutes on each side or until lightly browned.

3. Spoon the pineapple on to four plates. Top with the brioche slices, spoon over a little of the caramel sauce and add a dollop of crème fraiche.

Tall tales

In Summer a pile of berries makes a good substitute for the pineapple, or try some grilled peaches. The latter only need to be halved, dusted with sugar and flashed under the grill.

Belgian Waffle

115g all purpose flour
115g whole-wheat flour
1 tablespoon of sugar
2 teaspoons of baking powder
Pinch of salt
3 eggs
750ml milk
2 tablespoons vegetable oil

1. Put all the dry ingredients (flour, sugar, baking powder, and salt) into one bowl.

2. Put all the wet ingredients (eggs, milk, and oil) into another bowl and beat until the eggs and milk become one.

3. Pour the mix you've just made into the bowl with dry stuff and mix again, until there are no lumps left.

4. Now put half cup of batter you made in the hot waffle iron and cook until golden brown.

Banana waffle split and chocolate sauce

4 bananas
1 teaspoon cinnamon
1 tablespoon sugar
1 tablespoon plain flour

1. Peel banana, cut into halves.

2. Roll in cinnamon sugar coating.

3. Cook in cool fryer (175C) until golden. Drain off excess oil with kitchen paper.

4. Place the waffle on the plate topped with fried bananas halves. Serve topped with a vanilla ice cream ball. Drizzle hot chocolate sauce and butterscotch sauce on top.

Plum rum and ginger trifle

While we respect tradition at Giraffe, it is not something we feel comfortable with. At heart we are playful. Ask any giraffe. There is a willingness to try. We like to think our tall aspect allows us to gaze about and in so doing it is hard not to pick up ideas. Trifle is one of those good ideas stuck in a time warp. Why sherry when there are so many other good drinks around, rum being one of them. Plums are another and one good thing led to another...

400g fresh plums, halved and stoned
200ml water
75g crystallized ginger, chopped
200g sugar
1 cinnamon stick
Peel of 1 lemon
1 teaspoon star anise powder

400g sticky gingerbread cake
175g apricot jam
50ml dark rum
400g tin of ready made custard
200ml whipped cream

1. Combine the first five ingredients with the plums in a saucepan over a low heat and simmer until the plums just start to collapse. Allow to cool.

2. Spread the jam on the gingerbread cake. Stir the rum and custard into the cream.

3. You can either serve this as one trifle, very traditional, in a glass bowl or in individual glasses which gives it a slightly more modern feel perhaps, but also makes serving easier.

4. Layer the cake, plums and custard finishing with the custard. Allow to sit for an hour so the flavours infuse. Tradition dictates a large glass bowl, but a more modern interprietation is to use glasses, something with a stem or tumblers.

Tall tales

Other drinks to consider making trifle with:
Maderia
Amontillado, a sherry that delivers nuttiness but with a sweet edge
Vin Santo
Ginger wine – very English but rather good
Cointreau

Acknowledgements

Russel Joffe would like to thank his wife and business partner Juliette, his children Gideon, Mattea and Jemina for their support in helping build Giraffe into the business it is today and his partner Andrew Jacobs for helping him start the business in 1998 and giving him the time to put this book together. A special thank you to Darren Reilly for helping with the recipes.

Russel Joffe is the founder and CEO of Giraffe. He has worked in the restaurant business for over 30 years having worked in such places as Odette's, Coconut Grove and managing Langan's Brasserie in its early years. He launched his first business in 1984 called Le Bistroquet and started the Café Flo bistro chain in 1987, before founding Giraffe in 1998, which has now expanded all over the UK and is franchised in key locations in airports such as Heathrow and Manchester.

Hugo Arnold has written food columns in the London *Evening Standard*, the *Financial Times* and the *Irish Times*. He is a leading menu consultant to restaurant groups and is the author of eight books, including *Buying the Best* and *Outdoor Feasts*, *The Wagamama Cookbook* and *Wagamama 2: Ways with Noodles* and has won a Glenfiddich food award for his innovative writing.

First published in hardback in Great Britain in 2010
by Weidenfeld & Nicolson
an imprint of the Orion Publishing Group Ltd,
Orion House, 5 Upper St Martin's Lane,
London WC2H 9EA

An Hachette UK Company

10 9 8 7 6 5 4 3 2 1

A CIP catalogue record for this book is available from the British Library.

ISBN: 978 0 297 85662 7

Designed and illustrated by Sian Rance, D.R. ink
Photography by Deidre Rooney
Art directed by Natasha Webber
Edited by Jane Sturrock, Nicola Crossley and Clare Hacking
Index by Alan Thatcher

Printed and bound in China

The Orion Publishing Group's policy is to use papers that are natural,
renewable and recyclable and made from wood grown in sustainable forests.
The logging and manufacturing processes are expected to conform to the
environmental regulations of the country of origin.

www.orionbooks.co.uk